THE FAITH CODE

THE FAITH CODE

A FUTURE-PROOF FRAMEWORK FOR A LIFE OF MEANING AND IMPACT

TERRY BRISBANE
&
RUSTY RUEFF

with
RICK KILLIAN

Morehouse Publishing
NEW YORK

Unless otherwise indicated, scripture quotations are taken from *The Holy Bible, English Standard Version*, copyright © 2001 by Crossway Bibles, a division of Good News Publishers. Used by permission. All rights reserved.

Scripture quotations marked KJV are taken from the *King James Version* of the Bible.

Scripture quotations marked MSG are from *The Message* by Eugene H. Peterson, copyright © 1993, 1994, 1995, 1996, 2000, 2001, 2002. Used by permission of NavPress Publishing Group. All rights reserved.

Scripture quotations marked NASB are taken from the (NASB®) *New American Standard Bible*®, Copyright © 1960, 1971, 1977, 1995, 2020 by The Lockman Foundation. Used by permission. All rights reserved. www.lockman.org

Scripture quotations marked NKJV are taken from the *New King James Version* of the Bible. Copyright © 1979, 1980, 1982 by Thomas Nelson, Inc. Used by permission. All rights reserved.

Scripture quotations marked NLT are taken from *The Holy Bible, New Living Translation*, copyright © 1996. Used by permission of Tyndale House Publishers, Inc., Wheaton, Illinois, 60189. All rights reserved.

Manuscript prepared with Rick Killian, Killian Creative, Boulder, Colorado. KillianCreative.com

Morehouse Publishing, 19 East 34th Street, New York, NY 10016

Morehouse Publishing is an imprint of Church Publishing Incorporated.

Cover design by David Baldeosingh Rotstein
Typeset by Nord Compo

A record of this book is available from the Library of Congress.

ISBN 978-1-64065-655-0 (hardcover)
ISBN 978-1-64065-656-7 (ebook)

DEDICATIONS

FROM TERRY

To Sheryl
who could have known, dear wife of my youth and now passing
middle years, the journey with you would be so sweet . . .

FROM RUSTY

To my brother Tommy, you, who more than anyone I know
has lived out service, commitment, and personal sacrifice for
the good of others. I remain in awe.

FROM BOTH OF US

To those who are doing their best
with all that they have been given.

CONTENTS

"What do you benefit if you gain
the whole world but lose your own soul?"

—*Matthew 16:26* NLT

UNLOCKING THE FAITH CODE

"I came that they may have life and have it abundantly."

—John 10:10

There's an app for that.™

—Apple

The conversation that led to this book started over a decade ago. Three of us—the pastor of a church in the heart of San Francisco (Terry), a Silicon Valley C-suite guy (Rusty), and the president of a global nonprofit (our friend, David)—started meeting together at 7:00 AM every Wednesday morning at Ritual Coffee in the Mission District. This ritual has continued at various times and locations over the years as best we've been able to manage—other commitments, travel, and COVID-19 notwithstanding. The basic idea was this: We would get a coffee, talk about our lives, our ambitions, and our missions, and then pray together over whatever was on our hearts.

It was a step toward living the reason God put us on the earth and an admission that we needed a regular check-in to keep us on track. It was our hope that by committing to each other, being transparent, and agreeing together in prayer, we could experience the promise of *"As iron sharpens iron, so a friend sharpens a friend."*[1]

We wanted to be better people and grow in stewarding our responsibilities at the organizations where we had leadership roles. We wanted to learn from each other about what it means to live lives that are courageous, innovative, and meaningful. We wanted the world around us to be better for our having been in it. And so, despite challenges and other obligations trying to get in the way, we kept meeting, and we kept the conversation going.

As we've shared our aspirations, frustrations, and short-comings over the years, our conversations have often reflected the nature of living and working in the Bay Area. Here the very air we breathe is filled with collisions of faith, innovation, disruption, culture, and enterprise. In a lot of ways, San Francisco and Silicon Valley, good or bad, are on the leading edge of what our world is today and where it is going in the decades to come.

With each new technology and each cultural shift, we are forced to question much of what has gone before. Change often comes as fast as a new idea can be implemented, and often before the ramifications of it have been considered. Progress is good, in general, but there are also pitfalls. We know there are some things that don't change and never should. There are foundations that shouldn't be chipped away. There are truths that remain universal. There are things about being human that should be cultivated, and others that should be stifled. While we have great potential for good, human beings also have great potential for selfishly exploiting others—a sad truth that is reaffirmed with each news cycle—locally, nationally, and globally.

We have found that, while the world changes around us, foundational life topics such as calling and vocation, faith and purpose, ambition and character, and stewardship and influence—to name a few—need to be constantly reexamined and understood anew to keep us relevant and at the top of our games. It would be great if, in life as well as in work, we could attend a single weekend "discover your purpose" retreat and come away with a plan for life, but it just doesn't work like that. Our worlds—both inside and out—are just too complex and need constant adjustment and recalibration. God's plans for our lives demand growth. Who we are today is unlikely to be sufficient for tomorrow. The need to be able to pivot should never take us by surprise. We need instead to develop rhythms that keep us constantly cycling back to and through the things that matter the most, instead of simply charging ahead in one area while neglecting all others.

And so, again and again over the years, we've come back to the same questions in different forms: *Just what does it mean to live "a good life"? What should we be comfortable letting go of? And where should we be doubling down?*

We have come to believe that answering these questions demands constantly revisiting four phases of life—what we will call framework, design, perspective, and evaluation—on a regular basis.

> And so, again and again over the years, we've come back to the same questions in different forms: *Just what does it mean to live "a good life"? What should we be comfortable letting go of? And where should we be doubling down?*

First is the question of our *framework* for living lives of meaning and impact. There are so many pressures we face in life—how do we deal with them all? How do we show up as the best versions of ourselves and not get smothered by all the expectations and messaging of the world around us? How do we stay true to our commitments and promises without losing ourselves? How do we correctly handle the demands of our ambitions, our aspirations, and our callings? Whether you are building a business or a nonprofit, governing a city, state, or nation, or growing a family to maximize each member's potential, the default standards you are instilling and the culture you are creating support every behavior of each life you influence. Doing this right demands that you have an accurate sense of who you are and what you're about, as well as a worldview that promotes hope and communicates wisdom. Foundational principles, by definition, undergird every aspect and accomplishment of our daily lives. It's important to build on solid ground that is dependable and sure.

Once we have a handle on that framework, how do we use it to *build* our lives? How do we manage the days, weeks, and years that make up our lives? How do we—and our missions—grow through what we do every day? What rhythm do we establish to keep us anchored in what we value most? How do we make room for pivoting as we need to—whether it is to course correct or change our destination entirely?

To be effective, proper design demands proper *application*. So many things seem right until we step back to realize the bigger picture. We need help with our blind spots. What we don't know, what we don't see, what we don't recognize, *can* hurt us. What really is important? How do our current plans relate to things in the long run? How do we weather life's storms? Are we measuring the right things to get the right results, or are we majoring in the minors? What mindsets do we need to form, and which are holding us back?

And finally, how do we know if we're doing it right? We need proper *testing* to tell if we set our framework up correctly. What outcomes should we be experiencing in our day-to-day lives and interactions with others? What attitudes and attributes should be natural outflows of our doing life and work *right*? What fruit should we be bearing?

The more the three of us have discussed such questions, the more we've realized that each of us has an internal and an external world, a spiritual and a natural identity, a sense of who we are to *be* as well as what we are to *do,* and of how what we are *doing* doesn't count the same if it's not coming from the proper kind of *being*. It is in the tensions between these dichotomies that heaven and earth meet. It is in this intersection we believe the proper application of the faith code matters the most.

These are the perspectives from which we've tried to write in each chapter. As coauthors, we have tried to blend our voices, but still bring our own individual experiences and strengths forward. With this in mind, each chapter is organized into two parts, one from the spiritual perspective and the other from the natural—one from the faith code, if you will, and the other an application for it.

Each chapter begins with Terry exploring the internal or *being* side of a question, usually through a teaching or parable of Jesus. This is spiritual foundational material that should demonstrate the Original Designer's perspective and intent. We believe that only by first interacting with the principles for living that Jesus used to "disrupt" his world can we get an understanding of how we are to influence our own times, unique challenges, and relationships.

After that, Rusty will take us from Sunday into Monday (or whenever your work week begins) and the lives we live outside the church doors—what we *do* from who we *are*. Just how do the foundations, perspectives, and principles set forth in God's Word apply to the world that challenges us every day? How do we use them to make our world a better place? Just how do we walk out our faith, hope, love, and heart's callings in a world that is at its best difficult, if not often downright hostile? How do we as women and men of faith live more justly, most joyfully, more closely and humbly with God, and more responsively to the needs and aspirations of others?

We believe life was meant to be an adventure—a sweep-you-off-your-feet love story and a journey of wonder, accomplishment, and strategic disruption of a culture that still hasn't figured how to love our neighbors as ourselves. We believe each of us is destined to face great challenges that we were meant to overcome. We are called to love, create, innovate, and revolutionize, and also to grow, nurture, and experience the wonder of each moment. God intended us to have relationships that are fulfilling and synergistic—that we be able to connect more sincerely with other human

> We are called to love, create, innovate, and revolutionize, and also to grow, nurture, and experience the wonder of each moment.

beings and be the better for it. We are meant to finish our races well and be recognized for our contributions. We don't subscribe to FOMO—"Fear Of Missing Out"—as a driver; we reside instead with YOLO—"You Only Live Once"—as a mantra. None of these things are accomplished unless we are swimming against the currents typical of our world. None of them happen if we just go with the flow.

Ours are incredible times. The world has changed as much in the first few decades of the twenty-first century as it did in all of the twentieth, and the changes we will see in the coming years will transform the world even further. According to Peter Diamandis and Steven Kotler, authors of *The Future Is Faster Than You Think*, "We're going to experience a hundred years of technological progress over the next ten years."[2] What is possible today with a smartphone boggles the capacity of the room-sized super computers that helped put men on the moon. Technology is creating breakthroughs faster than we have ever experienced in history. There has never been a time when so much was accessible to so many, nor when the disparities have been greater. Truly, we are only limited by our own imagination and ingenuity as to what we can accomplish—and the world needs us more than ever to be responsible, thoughtful, and loving in the way that we show up in it. We are the builders of the future, but if we are going to make tomorrow better than yesterday, we need a better way to do business, connect our communities, and govern our nations than we have right now.

So we invite you to join us in our coffeehouse-table conversations trying to figure out how to make the most of the life, gifts, and desires God has given each of us. We don't claim to be any more than we are—a pastor and a tech business guy—bringing forward our own experiences, trying to live a life of love for God and others, trying to stay faithful to the missions we've been called to, and be the changes we've been put on the earth to be.

With this in mind, we'd like to invite you to take this book and invite two friends to read it with you. (No pressure if you can't, but it's easier for it to be a conversation if you're not alone.) As we have done, we suggest connecting once a week to discuss the questions each chapter presents, share your thoughts and aspirations, and then pray together for whatever is on your hearts. It is sincerely our hope that joining this conversation will be as rewarding for you as it has been for us.

With that, we're so glad you've decided to join us. Do you have your coffee (or beverage of choice)?

Great! Let's dig in.

Pastor Terry Brisbane & Rusty Rueff
April 2023

PART I

THE FRAMEWORK

"These words I speak to you are not incidental additions to your life, homeowner improvements to your standard of living. They are foundational words, words to build a life on."

—*Matthew 7:24* MSG

ONE

THE FAITH CODE

> "But if you just use my words in Bible studies and don't work them into your life, you are like a stupid carpenter who built his house on the sandy beach. When a storm rolled in and the waves came up, it collapsed like a house of cards."
>
> —*Matthew 7:26–27* MSG

From the gold rush to tech start-ups, people have flocked to the Bay Area looking to make their fortunes and a name for themselves, quite often risking everything to do so. It is a place where businesses can emerge from a single idea and industries can crumble overnight because of a new technological breakthrough. For every Instagram-like unicorn,* there are a dozen MySpace cautionary tales.

---

* A company that goes from zero to a billion dollars in value.

No wonder VUCA has become a trendy managerial acronym—ours is certainly a volatile, uncertain, complex, and ambiguous world.

Because of this, from time to time, Rusty and I have a very similar conversation with people at different extremes. It tends to go something like this: Someone becomes part of a start-up, and in the whirlwind, roller-coaster world of Silicon Valley, discovers their company has latched onto an idea that customers love. Their business will soon be launching them beyond their wildest dreams. They are making ridiculous amounts of money, gaining notoriety, and at the same time, supporting the livelihoods and well-being of hundreds of employees and their families.

The realization gives them pause.

They come to one of us, looking for perspective. They ask something along the lines of, "What am I supposed to do? How is this going to change me? How will it affect my family? What will it do to my reputation? To my relationship with God?"

On the other hand, we've encountered some who started a company that did well for a time, but they are now realizing it's going to crash. It might just be bad timing, the wrong economy, a competitor beat them to market, an innovation has already made them obsolete, or they are facing insurmountable problems with execution. Articles are being written about their imminent demise, and not only are they facing financial ruin, but they're about to take a cadre of good people, people who have been faithful and loyal since the beginning, down with them.

When they come looking for answers, they ask, "What am I supposed to do? How is this going to change me? How will it affect my family? What will it do to my reputation? To my relationship with God?"

Yes, at both ends of the spectrum, if they are mindful, people are confronted with similar questions. What are they supposed to do in the face of immense pressure, be it from success or from failure? What will keep them grounded, keep their egos in check (or afloat), and how will they hold tight to what is truly important in the midst of one of life's major storms? How do they hang onto the best they can be and not let circumstances define or completely derail them?

One way to look at it might be to put it in the context of a quote from the Greek mathematician and inventor, Archimedes, who is credited with saying, "Give me a lever and a place to stand, and I will move the earth." What these people are asking when they come to Rusty or me is something along the lines of "I have my lever, and I'm about to move my world, but where do I stand to keep this great enterprise from rolling back over the top of me and crushing the very reason God put me on the earth?"

Just what is the "place to stand" from which we are supposed to "move the earth"—or "make our dent in the universe" as Steve Jobs so famously said? What is the firm ground—the most stable and secure foundation—upon which we can build a life of flourishing, fulfillment, justice, significance, and love? What is the right framework for living an authentic life of meaning and impact?

DEFINING THE PARAMETERS
FOR "THE GOOD LIFE"

In three quick chapters early in the book of Matthew, Jesus discusses the parameters for creating this kind of life. He discusses the importance of certain attitudes, the power of our influence, anger, lust, divorce, dealing with enemies, judging others, anxiety, our relationship with wealth and possessions, our innate desires for recognition and fame, hypocrisy, and what is and isn't trustworthy in the world, as well as other challenges that plague the human soul. The passage has come to be commonly referred to as the Sermon on the Mount.[1]

In one of the first books of the Bible, shortly after God rescued the people of Israel from lives of slavery in Egypt, God gave them the Ten Commandments. I realize that, for some of us, those might seem archaic. After all, "Thou shalt not . . ." hardly comes across as liberating. But when we view them that way, I think we are missing a key point. It was really intended as a law of liberty.

These commandments were not just "rules" to live by, but introduced a nation with a slave mentality to a new way of thinking. The only cultural identity the Israelites knew at that point was formed from generations of being slaves. God was not just delivering them from physical bondage, but also from emotional and spiritual captivity. He gave them these ten life principles as what would become his law for living as God's chosen people on the earth.

They were characteristics that would set them apart from every other nation around them. They were not restrictions

6

so much as a gift. Almost like a constitution, the commandments gave them a framework for their social, moral, religious, and national life, and contained the keys to God's original intent for how human beings would find meaning and fulfillment in their relationships and work on the earth.

At the beginning of his ministry, Jesus does something very similar. He takes on several accepted religious and cultural practices and discusses the true bedrock beneath them. In many ways it's a deepening of the Ten Commandments, taking law and showing its spiritual undergirding. He's teaching principles that will define the identity of those who follow him.

Repeatedly Jesus proclaims, "You have heard it said . . ., but I say unto you. . . ." He lays out an accepted cultural-religious norm that has come out of interpretations of God's Old Testament commandments and then redefines it according to the Original Designer's intention. His sayings hit home because they are based on something planted deep within each person—not on what is *permissible*, but what is truly *living* as God would have each of us live. He looks not to the exterior actions alone, but to what these actions say about what is in the person's heart and express about the health of their spiritual connection to God.

In each statement, Jesus essentially tells us, "This is what you have come to accept as the way the world works—and this is how you act as a result. But I'm telling you the truth is deeper. You think you are fine living like this, that it pleases God, but if you really want to live life as he designed it, your thoughts and actions must be founded on a better, more solid understanding of what he created the universe to be. In much of how you live, you're missing the point of what God intended. My Father's goal was that we might do every-thing from the same love he used to create us and the world we love, and that everything you set your hand to would flourish in the process."

> Jesus doesn't mince words as he changes the conversation from living according to moral laws and beliefs to doing everything from the context of God's love—from a place of deep relationship with him.

Jesus doesn't mince words as he changes the conversation from living according to moral laws and beliefs to doing everything from the context of God's love—from a place of deep relationship with him.

In the conclusion of this sermon, Jesus tells us:

> *Everyone then who* hears *these words of mine and* does *them will be like a wise man who built his house on the rock. And the rain fell, and the floods came, and the winds blew and beat on that house, but it did not fall, because it had been founded on the rock.*

> *And everyone who* hears *these words of mine and* does not do *them will be like a foolish man who built his house on the sand. And the rain fell, and the floods came, and the winds blew and beat against that house, and it fell, and great was the fall of it.*[2]

What Jesus is saying here is that the foundation of "the good life"—the kind of life God created us for and that he invites us into—is built on the rock-solid platform of two activities: (1) *hearing* his words and (2) then *doing* what they inspire us to do.

I believe *hearing* here also implies understanding, letting Jesus's words sink deep down into us to build our inner character and develop our personal convictions. *Doing* then expresses that transformation in correct and just actions evident to the world around us. By contrast, *hearing* and not being transformed and not *doing* both miss the point. It is building a life that looks good—that is a mere image—until the first big storm comes along and wipes everything out.

You might compare hearing (and not hearing) and doing (and not doing) in a 2x2 chart something like this:

	NOT DOING (INACTIVE LOVE)	DOING (ACTIVE LOVE)
HEARING JESUS'S WORDS (BUILDING SPIRITUAL CAPACITY)	BUILDING ON THE SAND	BUILDING ON THE ROCK
NOT HEARING JESUS'S WORDS (NOT BUILDING CAPACITY)	PASSIVELY LETTING THE WORLD AROUND US DICTATE OUR IDENTITY	TRYING TO "LOOK GOOD" DISCONNECTED FROM GOD'S LOVE AND SPIRITUAL STRENGTH

Hearing the words of Jesus in the form of reading the Bible (or listening to it), hearing his teachings unpacked through sermons in a church service, on a podcast, or through a blog or book, and so forth is a discipline we all should carry on throughout the week. It keeps what is important in front of us. It instructs our beliefs, values, and worldview. It tells us of God's love for us, of our adoption into his heavenly family, and about who we are to be in the world. James goes so far as to call scripture a mirror—something we look into to know who we really are:

> For if anyone is a hearer of the word and not a doer, he is like a man who looks intently at his natural face in a mirror. For he looks at himself and goes away and at once forgets what he was like. But the one who looks into the perfect law, the law of liberty, and perseveres, being no hearer who forgets but a doer who acts, he will be blessed in his doing.[3]

God told Joshua the way to *"make your way prosperous"* and *"have good success"* was to *"meditate on it* [God's law] *day and night"* and be *"careful to do according to all the law* [said to do]."[4] This was God's prescription for getting his principles inside of us and building our capability to stay true to his words throughout the week. When we act on what we are hearing, we exercise our faith and do "good" as Jesus taught and demonstrated.*

Notice that all who *hear* build beautiful houses. In many ways, it's impossible to tell the quality of one from the other. When life is good and all is smooth sailing, both houses look great. Both are wonderful places to live.

And, yes, most of the time things are fine or are going great and it's hard to imagine the seas will ever get rough.

---

* Note that I'm not putting good works over faith here, but good works as an expression of faith. It is not the works that justify us, but our relationships to God as his daughters and sons. Through spiritual disciplines, our faith grows, and thus also our capacity to do good in the world. You can't really have one without the other.

Overall, we live in one of the most prosperous times the world has ever experienced, though it's not without its challenges. (We need to look no further than COVID-19 and recent economic crises—not to mention the war in Ukraine—to be reminded of that.) Inevitably, storms *will* come, and when they hit with compounding force, even the strongest among us will be shaken. When the storm comes, one house will collapse and the other will protect those who live in it against the wind, the rain, and the cold.

That is why Jesus said it matters what we do with that we hear—the framework we build our lives on matters. What we do is a huge part of what forms us as human beings and ultimately makes us who we are. So it matters what we choose as our foundation for what we do on a daily basis. Building on the wrong things sets us up for collapse down the road.

I like how Luke phrases this same parable: he adds that the builder "*dug deep and laid the foundation on the rock.*"[5] That represents the serious digging—the deep internal work—that needs to be done to live the lives God promises his faithful, despite the natural hardships of living in a tumultuous, VUCA world.

Who we become as we follow Jesus really is an inside job. We're getting his words and sayings and digging deep to lay them as the bedrock beneath all our actions. His words are character forming and identity defining. The firm foundation of our lives begins by hearing who Jesus tells us that we are and believing his voice over all the other voices vying to define us. When we act on an identity based in being adopted into his family—as his beloved sons and daughters called as benevolent builders of his kingdom on the earth—we grow stronger. Our foundational principles reinforce themselves. *Hearing* and *doing* form how we interact with the world, because we are not trying to pull our sense of purpose, value, and meaning from the world and how others say we are, but instead reform our world to look more like what God created it to be as expressions of who we are following Jesus.

> The firm foundation of our lives begins by hearing who Jesus tells us that we are and believing his voice over all the other voices vying to define us.

Finding a solid and stable foundation for your life isn't a one and done activity. While there are a lot of "find your purpose in life" books and workshops that are all worth their time, they are never enough. Identity is not built in a day, nor does it remain the same over a lifetime. Who we are is constantly growing and changing between the forces of internal and external pressures. Who we are depends on how we speak and react to the world around us according to the intentions of our heart and the capacity of our character.

In his book, *Sources of the Self*, philosophy professor Charles Taylor writes:

My identity is defined by the commitments and identifications which provide the frame or horizon within which I can try to determine from case to case what is good, or valuable, or what ought to be done, or what I endorse or oppose. In other words, it is the horizon within which I am capable of taking a stand.[6]

It can't be said enough that who we want to become in life can only be determined from what we have established that life upon. Where we stand determines how much leverage we have to "move the earth," as Archimedes so aptly put it. As people consciously choosing to be a force for good, that begins with continuously hearing God's Word and living it out with others into the world around us.

WE NEED A PROPER FRAMEWORK

As Terry (switching to Rusty, here) just laid out so well, we need to build our lives on something solid and resilient if we are going to survive the ups and downs of life. Life is heavy. We know that. Life is ever-changing. We know that too. If only for these reasons, we can't build the life we desire without establishing it with something solid. And we will never realize our full potential if we don't work hard on keeping our foundation strong and always ready to support what will be new or necessary. We need a time-tested and always-true framework to make life fully come together.

So, how are you doing on that?

Since ancient times, philosophers and theologians have tried to figure out questions to help unpack that very process of becoming a person of quality and influence capable of living a significant and fulfilling life—a life where we build something noteworthy, but do not lose ourselves in the process. They are the basic questions of existence: Who am I? Why am I here? What is meaningful? What is "the good life"? And given these things, how then should I live?

I like how philosophy and theology professor James K. A. Smith sums this up in his book, *You Are What You Love*, basically with one question:

> Jesus doesn't . . . ask, "What do you know?" He doesn't ask, "What do you believe?" He asks, "What do you want?" This is the most incisive, piercing question Jesus can ask of us precisely because we are what we want. Our wants and longings and desires are at the core of our identity, the wellspring from which our actions and behavior flow. Our wants reverberate from our heart, the epicenter of the human person. Thus Scripture counsels, "Above all else, guard your heart, for everything you do flows from it" (Proverbs 4:23). Discipleship, we might say, is a way to curate your heart, to be attentive and intentional about what you love.[7]

So let me ask you this: "What do you love?" And I don't mean what do you think you should love, but given a typical day and how you show up in it, "What *do* you love?"

In my own life, I have to admit, I have many "loves." Let me list some I have had over the course of my lifetime. I have loved, or currently love, in no particular order:

My friends	Serving on boards	Teaching children
My Tesla	of directors for	Sex
My wife, Patti	businesses and	Reading
My work	nonprofits	Being stylish
My dog, Theo	Live theater	(at least my style)
Watching TV	Working on	Going to church
Running	politics	Writing

Being healthy
Hosting radio
  shows or podcasts
Being "in the
  know"
Having people
  look up to me
Being a Purdue
  alum

Being generous
The SF Giants
  and the Golden
  State Warriors
Going on vacations
  with my wife
Golf
Having the
  financial freedom

to do many
  things I want
My mother and
  brother
Growing up in
  Indiana
Jesus

I could go on, but I think you get the picture. These things that I have loved over the years are what make me *me*. They are what give me a place to stand out from everyone else in the world as well as a place to belong and a sense of significance, character, contribution, and capability within a community surrounding me. They are what allow me to fit in, but also to be unique. Whether I like it or not, what I love is what has formed my identity since the day I was born.

Identity is a funny thing. It forms whether we pay attention to it or not, just beneath the surface in our unconscious minds. If I had to define it, I would say identity is a force in our life that is refined in the crucible between inner desires and outer expectations, responsibility, and messaging. It determines both how we think of ourselves on the inside and how we show up in the world on the outside. If I were going to draw a diagram of it, it might look something like the diagram on the next page.

There are internal influences that make us unique: gifts and talents, aspirations and dreams, desires, among other things we characterize as attributes God has implanted within us, perhaps from birth. But the world around us also

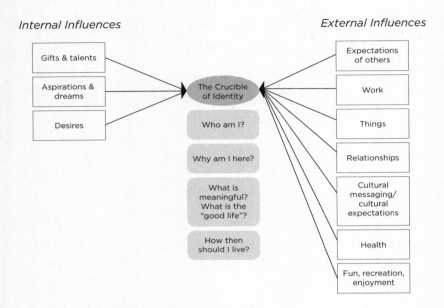

Gifts & talents

Aspirations & dreams

Desires

The Crucible of Identity

Who am I?

Why am I here?

What is meaningful? What is the "good life"?

How then should I live?

Expectations of others

Work

Things

Relationships

Cultural messaging/ cultural expectations

Health

Fun, recreation, enjoyment

has a lot to say about who we should be: There are expectations, responsibilities, socioeconomic conditions, relationships, possessions, and so on, as well as all kinds of voices telling us what we should want, how to be healthy and live "right," what we should stand for and against, and so much more. You and I, with our constant questions about what the best way is to exist, are caught in the crossfire trying to find the answers we need—trying to figure out who we really are.

Not only that, but we have a deep desire to be "seen." We want people to recognize us for who we are—to know us—and to acknowledge that we have a unique contribution to make to the world around us. In these things, we also want to be loved—intimately, by those closest to us, and through respect, by our societies. And we are constantly looking for what it is that gives us worth.

I like what Sanyin Siang, of the Coach K Center on Leadership & Ethics at Duke University, said about identity when I helped interview her on the *Faith Driven Entrepreneur* podcast a couple of years ago: "Identity is so key. Unless we are intentional about who we want to be and what matters, we can easily get distracted by all these things that are not true to our identity, but we think they are."[8]

It's as if our subconscious creates a scorecard to justify feeling good about ourselves as human beings from the day we are born. First, we matter if our parents love us, if we have friends at school, if we do well in class, if we master a sport or a game, or are good at a craft or art or any of a number of other things as we grow up. As a rule, we go for the low-hanging fruit (and if we don't find things to tell us we matter, we experience trauma that can be debilitating, but let's leave that for later and keep it in the positive for now).

We matter because of the things that make us stand out and put us near the top—the fastest runner, the highest grades, the best at drawing spaceships, the cutest, the most popular, or whatever. These are the things that make us feel good about ourselves, but we also don't generally give too much conscious thought to, because if we did, we might realize how shallow and fragile our identities really are.

As we live into our twenties, thirties, forties, and beyond, it's easy not to grow out of picking from the low-hanging fruit and defining ourselves by noteworthy external characteristics or what gives us little jolts of affirmation. Since we spend most of our waking hours in the week working, it's easy to allow that world to have the greatest influence in determining how we see ourselves. Yes, we are what we value and believe—what we hear and internalize as Jesus seemed to be saying—but more significantly, we are what we *do*. Intentions are important, but they don't always overshadow our actions. What we continually *do* has a way of determining who we *become*. It's a process that, if we don't step back and take control of it, can take us places in life we never expected—or ever wanted—to go.

As a case in point, let me tell you a personal story.

In 1998, my wife, Patti, and I made a left-hand turn when I left PepsiCo in New York and joined an emerging video gaming company called Electronic Arts (EA) in Silicon Valley. Patti had the longer PepsiCo career and was arguably more successful as she ascended from the "steno pool"* without a college education to becoming the executive assistant to Roger Enrico, the CEO and chairman of PepsiCo. (He was a marketing legend—he was the one who signed Michael Jackson to Pepsi before music celebrities did advertising.) When I left PepsiCo for my new career adventure, Patti also left her career behind. (She loved me and the life we were building together more. She was getting something right that I soon learned I was taking for granted.)

While Patti tried to settle into the somewhat siloed culture of Silicon Valley, I worked and worked and worked. I felt I

---

* *Steno* is short for "stenographer," people who used to come into an executive's office to take shorthand dictation and then type it up. The fact that you've probably never heard of such a thing is a perfect metaphor for how fast technology changes things, don't you think?

had to establish myself (read "my identity") in an industry I knew nothing about with people who knew nothing about me. As developer and entrepreneur John Marsh said on a recent episode of *Faith Driven Investor*, "Identity drives behavior."[9] I, naturally, wanted my identity to be that I was a valuable asset to my company, and that identity became the core of everything I did because it was all I saw as giving me worth.

Every day I felt I needed to exhibit my value to the company and get enough "wins" to prove that they had made the right decision hiring me. (A pretty natural feeling for most of us in work, I am sure.) And if I am being fully transparent, I really "loved" my job. And all of that was just fine—for a while.

About a year into the job, on a typical weeknight, Patti and I were sitting on the couch together, "watching" TV to the nightly background soundtrack of clicking laptop keys as I answered email. If Patti said something, I responded with "Uh huh," "Right," or "Sure, whatever you think," while I focused on my "important" work. It had become my MO, but I was home rather than at the office, and that had to count for something, right?

Well, not as much as I thought.

In the midst of who knows what we were watching, Patti said, "I think I'm going to go back to New York."

"Oh, what for?" I said, hardly looking up. My first thought was that someone in her family might be ill. My second was that she wanted to spend some time with friends for some occasion or event that I had forgotten. I was off by a mile.

"To live," she said.

Then I looked up.

It was only by the grace of God that I had enough sense not to counterargue, but to close my laptop and put it aside so I could genuinely listen.

It was a wake-up moment for me.

Thankfully she didn't go back to New York, and wisely I stopped "click, click, clicking" away every night (not perfectly by any means, there were still those "have to" times, but those were no longer the norm).

As we might describe it according to what Terry said above, I was *hearing* at church, I just wasn't *doing* according to what I was hearing. I was doing something else, and it was making me someone other than who I wanted to be. Thankfully, I got better at doing the right things—really quickly! What I had messed up was not only my priorities but also the framework I was using to build my life.

In Silicon Valley where I spent most of my career—like the games we built at EA—entire worlds are built from software code. As products develop, we recognize that there is good code and bad code—code that makes things work and code that makes things break or crash. For computers, smartphones, tablets, and so on there is operating code (Windows, Linux, AppleOS, iOS, Android, etc.) and there are applications (apps) that run on that foundational code. The better the foundational code is, the better the apps run, and generally the less energy they need to function.

The most important code, though, is even deeper—what is often referred to as "source code." Source code is structural code upon which everything else is built. It creates the framework—a skeleton—upon which devices function and applications run. It tends to be seen as the very lifeblood of a technology company. It is guarded as a trade secret. It is fought over in intellectual property courts. It is the goose that lays golden eggs. Without it, or if it was somehow stolen and shared with the world, the company could well cease to exist. (As I am typing this, it is in the news that some of Twitter's source code was posted in a public forum and its lawyers fought to have it taken down. Twitter's CEO, Elon Musk, estimated that the value of the company more than halved, from the $44 billion he paid for it to about $20 billion, as a result of their source code being "leaked.")

At the same time, code is simply language. It is "words" that create instructions that not only tell a computer how to run, what to show on the screen, and how to react to inputs, but also determine its purpose and define everything it does. Programs don't do things that weren't first created in their code (at least, not yet). Even artificial intelligence programs and large language models like ChatGPT don't create out of thin air but scour oceans of data to learn and create from the data they've processed. All of technology is based on laws, rules—"commandments," if you will—that determine how they operate in the world. For any program to do a new thing it didn't do in the past, it needs to be recoded in some way—either rewritten or have something added to the code it "lived by" before.

This got me to thinking. What if we approached Jesus's words to us as "the ultimate source code" for building our lives on the rock he talks about in the Sermon on the Mount? What if the Bible and what it says about who we are and how we are to live became the code for "writing" our individual lives on the earth? What if we lived with constant subroutines of God's Word running beneath the surface of our every action and interaction as we went about our days?

I know that's a little superficial. We are much more complex than computers, even as computers and programming become more complex every day. But what if that were a place to start? What if we could use *hearing* Jesus's words and *doing* what they implied as a basic framework for life? What if we based our identities on them and let them determine not only what we love, but how we love?

Despite what I was hearing at church, the code I was living by at home with Patti was not God's source code, but the code I was getting from the office. It wasn't even something that was stated, but something I had perceived and adopted without any real consideration. I was taking a secondary love (work) and prioritizing it over a primary love (my wife). I was taking the energy I should have been applying in my marriage and letting it get sucked up in the nonessentials of my work. (I mean, did every email sent to me really need such a detailed answer?) I wasn't running my life from my internal convictions, but on default worldly priorities—I was hoping my actions would some day in the future result in a pat on the back from my boss rather than being with my wife *who was right there in the moment with me*. That's not to say work is bad or can't be very rewarding and fulfilling, but I had it out of place. I wasn't running my life by the values I espoused—if you'd asked me, I would have said my marriage was more important—but I was defaulting to pecking away at my keyboard like a bird in a Skinner box trying to get food. I was getting caught up in the currents of life around me, and if I didn't change course, as soon as we hit turbulent waters, I was likely to end up in a life raft alone.

To go back to the crucible of identity illustration, the source code of Jesus's words to us is both an external and an internal influence—or you could say they are external words we internalize to rewrite how we see ourselves and the way we want to live. The more we get them on the inside, the more we have the conviction to do them on the outside. The more we realize through them how much God loves us, the less important the "love" of the world becomes—the less "people-pleasing" we need to be. And the more we act according to this source code on the outside, the less likely our houses are to fall when a storm comes.

And since the Bible tells us we must live by faith, rather than calling it "source code," let's call it "faith code"—the code that builds the faith* inside of us necessary to show up in the world and fulfill the reasons God created us and put us on the earth.

To go back to our chart, you could look at it this way:

---

* Terry here: a good verse to think of for this is Romans 10:17, "*So faith comes from hearing, and hearing through the word of Christ.*"

The Framework

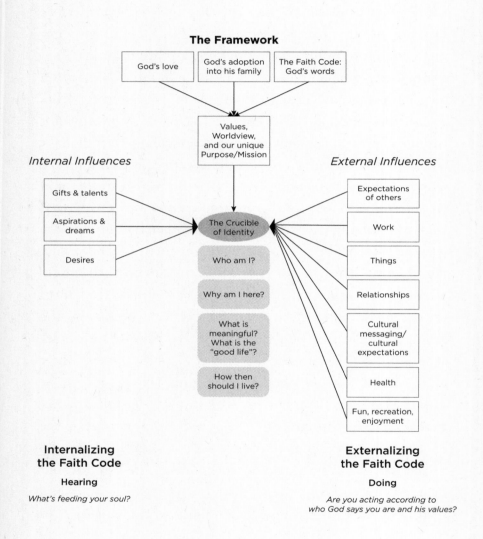

God's love

God's adoption into his family

The Faith Code: God's words

Values, Worldview, and our unique Purpose/Mission

Internal Influences

Gifts & talents

Aspirations & dreams

Desires

The Crucible of Identity

Who am I?

Why am I here?

What is meaningful? What is the "good life"?

How then should I live?

External Influences

Expectations of others

Work

Things

Relationships

Cultural messaging/ cultural expectations

Health

Fun, recreation, enjoyment

Internalizing the Faith Code

Hearing

What's feeding your soul?

Externalizing the Faith Code

Doing

Are you acting according to who God says you are and his values?

24

God's Word tells the story of our relations to him over thousands and thousands of years. It tells us how he chose a people to whom to send his son so that the whole world might be offered salvation. Through the context of history from the day of creation, on several levels, the Bible lays out how God has always loved us, how he is always for us, how sending Jesus allowed us to become members of his family, and how each of us has been given a calling to walk with him and spread his love. We are thus "children of God," but also "people of the Book." We are part of a family, brothers and sisters with unique contributions to make to each other both inside and outside of that family. We each have a great adventure to live and grow into, guided by what we choose to love and how well we love it.

Jesus came to the earth because God loves us.* Love is an action—something we *do*—with emphatic effort. I do things I love at a different quality level than things I like. If we don't choose what and how we will love, we will default to letting external forces tell us what to love—we will conform to what feeds our egos or tickles our fancies. We get sucked in by what makes us

> If we don't choose what and how we will love, we will default to letting external forces tell us what to love—we will conform to what feeds our egos or tickles our fancies.

* Terry again: From what is probably the most well-known verse in the Bible: *"For God so loved the world, that he gave his only Son, that whoever believes in him should not perish but have eternal life"* (John 3:16). The verse right after it is good too: *"For God did not send his Son into the world to condemn the world, but in order that the world might be saved through him"* (John 3:17).

feel special, important, or recognized. It's a trap. We look for approval (think "likes" on social media) when we are not sure that we are someone worthwhile on the inside, or we sink into escapism through some dopamine-fueled pleasure to avoid our feelings of inadequacy. We forsake those that are closest to us (like our time with God or evenings with our spouses and families) looking for satisfaction in something superficial. By doing so, we form our identities in totally backward ways, forsaking what is important for delusion.

You might have found it strange, for example, that I had "sex" on my list of loves at the beginning of this section (believe me, it felt weird to include it), but it's a part of life we all share. When I run sex according to God's faith code—within the boundaries of marriage and as God designed it—it feeds my life, but when I run it according to unharnessed desire, objectifying and dehumanizing others through pornography or some other lesser version of how sex was intended, I'm setting myself up for a major crash. The first is real and satisfying, but difficult; the second is easy and instantaneous, but eats away at our souls. One leads to life and life more abundantly; the other, most certainly, does not.

That's just one area, but I hope you are already seeing broader implications. It's the old adage that computer programs use as well: "Garbage in, garbage out." Just like your body needs nutritious food and exercise to be healthy, so does your soul.

So, as you might already be guessing, the "journey" we are asking you to take with us in this book is not for those who want to go with the flow or quickly scroll through life. The framework for living Terry and I are suggesting in these pages takes a great deal of self-awareness and self-examination. It demands real vulnerability and accountability to others we trust and respect. It's easy to get the "apps" of life messed up, out of order, and to lose sight of what is foundational because we are operating on corrupted code. It's easy to let the superficial define us and sneak into the upper echelons of our "I love" categories—how much money we make, the values of the company we founded, a job title, how popular we are among our colleagues, how many followers we have on social media, even how well our beloved sports teams do— rather than the true quality of our relationship with God, our closest friends and loved ones, and actively partnering with God in the purpose for which he put us on the earth.

Take it from me, once our loves get "out of whack," we can find ourselves totally lost, dazed, and confused. When we hit such an identity crisis, it can feel like the ground beneath our feet has disappeared. We suddenly don't know where we stand, and we question who we are. We are not our jobs, we are not our companies, we are bigger than our successes or failures. We are people put on the earth by God for a reason, and there is no greater fulfillment than partnering with God to accomplish that purpose.

So let's come up with a plan together that will keep us from losing who we really are. To do that, we need to plug regularly into the "faith code" with others we trust, but we also need one other thing. We need to tap into what powers the faith code—what makes Jesus's words more than just words, but light and sustenance. We need to plug into the very thing that powers the creation of an abundant life.

REFLECTION QUESTIONS

1. If the camera on your mobile device could take a picture of you being your true self, living your true values, what image would it capture?

2. In your own words, what is the "rock" Jesus taught us to build a successful life upon? How are you "building on that rock"? (Or not?) How should that affect your goals, focuses, and priorities from this day forward?

3. Read Matthew 5–7. What do you feel is Jesus's overall message in these chapters? What do you feel his words are calling you to? Where do they just feel like commandments, and where do they feel like spirit and life?

4. Name some things you love (and we mean besides the "right answers" like "reading my Bible," "praying," and "going to church"—let's just say those are givens). How do you love them? Are there things you would change about how you relate to them after reading this chapter? What do you plan to do differently going forward?

5. What are some of the most significant influences, internal and external, that contribute to your identity? How do they relate to who you want to become in the years ahead? Is there anything you should move to the "home screen" of your life to make it more prominent? Is there anything you should move off, maybe even delete?

TWO

———

THE POWER SOURCE

God is love, and whoever abides in love
abides in God, and God abides in him.

—1 John 4:16

I (Terry) was recently heading home after a series of planning meetings down the Peninsula (the stretch of land sandwiched between San Francisco and what was once noted as Silicon Valley—today Silicon Valley is thought of as extending to San Francisco proper), and I found myself passing my old high school, a place where profound moments altered the landscape of my life. I hadn't been there in decades, and I felt the urge to park and take a walk down memory lane. While much had changed, a lot had not, including the central courtyard where I remember sitting and pondering some of the big questions of life.

I committed to an ongoing relationship with Jesus Christ during the summer after my freshman year. When I returned to school as a sophomore—and for the rest of my time in high school—I often sat in that courtyard during my lunch hour, reading my Bible and contemplating Jesus's teachings, wondering what it meant for me and my future. School, sports, and family obligations took up most of my waking hours in those years, so the one time I had almost completely to myself was during lunch.

It was in the midst of such reading times that I realized if I was serious about following Jesus (and I was), I would need to learn more about what the scriptures taught. Revisiting the spot where I had spent so many lunchtimes, I remembered how I'd made the decisions to pursue God first with my time, then through my thought life, and eventually with my "real life" by going into the ministry and becoming a pastor.

High school certainly wasn't any different for me than anyone else. There were so many identity things to "worry" about: my changing body, peer pressure, and the human longing to love and be loved, and it's no wonder so many of us remember our teen years with mixed emotions. The best of times, the worst of times, as the saying goes.

However, the thing I remember the most of those years was how the Bible came alive and became central to everything I wanted out of life. I remember at one point reading the Old Testament book of Ecclesiastes. I started to compare its sayings with what Jesus taught in the Gospels. I also contrasted these teachings with the adolescent angst and drama my fellow students were experiencing. I saw a lot of parallels.

Solomon (the author of Ecclesiastes) taught about a very different kind of success than most of my peers were pursuing. Solomon called the human pursuit for pleasure and accomplishment "vanity": *"Then I considered all that my hands had done and the toil I had expended in doing it, and behold, all was vanity and a striving after wind."*[1] Real success is what lasts, what means something. I didn't comprehend then that Jesus was inviting me to "do" life differently—that he was giving me a map, a blueprint, for how life is supposed to be lived, on what it is supposed to be built, and the difference each of our lives is supposed to make. Choosing to follow that map instead of the one I was being offered by those around me was the best decision I've ever made.

As Jesus advised in Matthew 7:24, I decided to become a hearer and doer of his Word. That high school courtyard came to represent taking time to read my Bible and contemplate what God put me on the earth to accomplish. It was there I first asked myself, "If I were going to build my life on one thing, what would it be?"

FINDING YOUR "CENTER COURT"

This is, in essence, the same question Jesus was asked by a scribe in Mark 12:28. It is, I believe, the greatest conversation recorded in the Bible.

His question was simply: *"Which commandment is the most important of all?"*[2]

A scribe is a religious lawyer—someone who'd spent his education and career studying the Hebrew scriptures trying to determine the best way to live. He would have been someone who had tremendous knowledge of the regulations, nuances, and customs associated with the law of Moses.

We know that much like we experience in the US today, there were two predominant "parties" in the Jewish leadership of Jesus's times. It's important to remember that when Jesus walked the earth, Israel was not autonomous. Most of the known world in Europe, Near Asia, and much of North Africa was ruled by Rome. Through the significant weight of their military might, Rome bestowed on their occupied lands the *Pax Romana*: "the peace of Rome." They kept it with an iron fist.

Israel didn't like submitting to Rome, paying their taxes to Caesar, and living with soldiers walking their streets and demanding whatever they wanted of people. Life under the Romans was humiliating. On the other hand, Rome didn't want to fight a rebellion. It would cost too much in lives and resources. So they granted Israel's proxy king and religious leaders a degree of autonomy that was unique. Beneath the Roman governor and laws, they allowed the Jewish people a sense of self-governance—a certain jurisdiction over the affairs of their religious properties, laws, and customs.

This leadership was divided largely between two groups, the Pharisees and the Sadducees. The Sadducees, who were a little less strict about adherence to the scriptures and more open to Roman philosophies, were slightly more powerful. They were also a bit wealthier. They held the intellectual heft in their culture, being more broadly educated. They were predominantly urbanites, many living in Jerusalem. They didn't have the same sacred regard for the scriptures that the Pharisees did. Being students of the scriptures and the laws of Moses, scribes would have lined up more with the Pharisees than the Sadducees.

Thus when Jesus got into a debate with the Sadducees on the subject of the resurrection of the dead, this scribe was all ears. While the Sadducees denied the resurrection, Jesus argued quite eloquently from the scriptures that it was real. Jesus impressed him. These Sadducees were men of letters, revered in the community, and here was an untrained, seemingly simple rabbi with a carpenter's background taking them to task and showing the holes in their teachings.

Seeing his knowledge, the scribe decided to ask Jesus a question. There were times when people would ask Jesus questions to try to trip him up and make him look foolish (which never worked too well), but this wasn't one of them. I believe this scribe was sincere.

We don't know the scribe's name, but his question—oh, man—it is so good. This is such a great passage because it allows us to wrestle with the supreme issue of life. It gets straight to the heart of what's important and what gives life meaning.

Basically, he was asking, "I would like to get your opinion on what is the supreme duty of a human being. Where do you put the accent on living a fulfilling life? If you were to distill the laws of Moses down to their core, what would it be? What is the greatest principle we can obey as human beings to give our lives substance and meaning?"

Jesus's answer was just as direct and profound:

"The most important is, 'Hear, O Israel: The Lord our God, the Lord is one. And you shall love the Lord your God with all your heart and with all your soul and with all your mind and with all your strength.' The second is this: 'You shall love your neighbor as yourself.' There is no other commandment greater than these."[3]

Jesus didn't make this up off the top of his head. It comes from what the Jewish people call the *Shema Yisrael*, the central prayer of Judaism, which would roughly translate as "Listen, O Israel." Jesus's audience would have recognized the words as deeply rooted in the scriptures, specifically Deuteronomy 6:4–5: *"Hear, O Israel: The Lord our God, the Lord is one. You shall love the Lord your God with all your heart and with all your soul and with all your might."*

What Jesus was getting at was, "God desires us to love him in a way that is tender, in a way that is committed, in a way that is sincere, in a way that is intentionally thoughtful and utterly devoted." He was saying, "The first duty of every man and every woman is to acknowledge God, to truly acknowledge him, and to love him. Everything else emanates from that." He was giving us a peek at the "power source" of life and letting us know what our first love should be.

Jesus articulated this in a way that was both accessible and deeply compelling. And this would have been challenging enough. After all, what exactly does it mean *to love God*? It is a question worthy of a lifetime of contemplation. *What does it really look like to love God? And how do we make loving him the "center court" of our lives?*

Jesus didn't stop there, though. That wasn't enough. "Yes, love God, but there is one more thing as well." That one more thing came

> What does it really look like to love God? And how do we make loving him the "center court" of our lives?

from Leviticus 19:18, which says, *"You shall not take vengeance or bear a grudge against the sons of your own people, but you shall love your neighbor as yourself: I am the LORD."*

Hearing this, the scribe was intrigued. What Jesus said resonated him. Reading his response—you can feel the passion, the excitement—in his voice.

And the scribe said to him, "You are right, Teacher. You have truly said that he is one, and there is no other besides him. And to love him with all the heart and with all the understanding and with all the strength, and to love one's neighbor as oneself, is much more than all whole burnt offerings and sacrifices."[4]

What the young man was saying was, "Everything that we do at the temple—all the sacrifices, all the rules, all the rituals that we follow according to the law of Moses, all the religious things that we do and believe—these two commandments are greater *than all of those things*." You can imagine what that revelation must have been like to him—how excited it made him.

And Jesus got excited back. Look at how he responds. *"And when Jesus saw that he answered wisely, he said to him,*

'You are not far from the kingdom of God.'[5] Jesus was telling him, "You are so close! Your heart is open. Cultivate that; stay there. It will lead you to me like a lighthouse on the shore. The kingdom is before your very eyes. Take hold of it! And don't let go."

Because of their significance, together these have become known as "The Great Commandment."

This "Great Commandment" isn't just something we need to add to our to do lists: "I've got to log in my quiet time now—to love God a little—then I can get to the rest of my day." No, loving God and loving others as ourselves is the central activity for following Jesus. Everything we do should reflect that in some way, shape, or form. And more specifically, loving God heart, mind, soul, and strength is what anchors us in a storm—it is the rock, the platform, in many ways the core component of who we are and the solid ground we want to build our lives on.

In this, it's good to remember two things.

1. Loving God—as a daily practice—is the greatest thing we can ever do.

It is clearly no exaggeration to suggest that, for Jesus, rote obedience to legalistic principles and platitudes was not the goal. He was not interested in rule-based religion. That is not what the faith code is. As John wrote early in his Gospel: *"For the law was given through Moses; grace and truth came through Jesus Christ."*[6] The more I study Jesus's words and reflect on them, the more I feel him calling me past surface meanings into a deeper and more thoughtful way of life. Loving God is the source of spiritual strength and intelligence, and we see Jesus, time and again, finding a way to put spending time with his Father above all else.

The commandments, laws, precepts, and proverbs of the Bible have always been an attempt to describe what loving God looks like, not as behaviors unto themselves, but instead actions that express the nature of God the Father. Jesus was the walking, talking expression of that love and the nature of his Father. This is why getting to know him through reading about him in the Gospels is so important.

The Bible also tells us God desperately desires to share his love with us. When we love him, he reflects his love back to us. It's why he made the extravagant gesture of sending his one and only Son into this world. When we grasp how much we are loved, it calls for us to respond in kind, and then his love shines all the more. And being loved like that gives us the capacity and strength to take his love and love others in transformational ways.

2. Loving God and loving others are intertwined.

To say we love God and not the person next to us—someone who God created just as he created us—is a contradiction. A genuine and true love for God can't help but to radiate that love to others. It must show up in kindness and guardianship for everything God ever called "good," which is everything he has created (just see the first chapter of Genesis).

Jesus made it clear that love for God cannot be divorced from the realm of human relationship and stewardship of his creation. Loving God means living a life that is characterized by love and constantly "doing good"—doing things to make the world a more abundant, loving, just place. It is the light we shine to others: *"Let your light shine before others, so that they may see your good works and give glory to your Father who is in heaven."*[7]

First John 4:19 tells us: *"We love because he first loved us."* Jesus taught that human goodness that is not rooted in a love for God is, at best, a disconnected good, flowing only on a one-dimensional, human plane. It's like trying to grow a tree without roots. All true goodness flows from the God who endowed us with the capability to love like he does. Loving God is, in truth, what powers and makes sense of the faith code of the Bible. All love and goodness

> Loving God is, in truth, what powers and makes sense of the faith code of the Bible.

are maximized when we are connected to our Father and minimized when we are disconnected from the Creator of *"every good and perfect gift."*[8]

DRAWING FROM THE SOURCE

Thanks for that insight, Terry. It clearly shows why God's love is so important to living a flourishing, abundant life.

As I mentioned in the last chapter, in programming, the "source code" is the underlying architecture that makes a program or operating system work. It is what the programmer writes that is then compiled into the binary commands that make our devices function and our programs run. On one level, it is just row after row of commands, but, together, the effect is more than the sum of the parts. It gives the computer, tablet, or smartphone the instructions that allow them to "live" and do all the amazing things that they do.

Software programming is science, but it is also an art. There are those who can string together lines of code that produce remarkable results that others can't. There are those whose code is so intricate that others can't understand what the programmer was thinking. One programmer doesn't always understand another's code, even though they are writing in the same language. Computer applications have become so complex today that we have tasked smart machines and artificial intelligence to find better coding methodologies, or even develop new code on their own. There is also code that is so simple that it is remarkably intelligent and graceful.

Good code is coveted, and even worth stealing. Well-written, sophisticatedly structured code that works cleanly and doesn't sap too much energy is worth its weight in platinum! I can't think of a better way to describe the faith code that God has given us through the Bible—it is precious beyond measure.

In a brilliant move early in the history of Apple's iOS, they shared the source code of their operating system to allow others to use it as the basis for their own apps. This gave programmers the foundational architecture to create apps that would do anything they could imagine within the confines of the devices. Apple then centralized all of these apps into one vetted marketplace where it was simple to find an app for virtually any function you were looking for. This is what let Apple say, "There's an app for that!"™ It is one of the most brilliant business strategies of all time.

In the early days of this development, one of the most critical operating criteria Apple used for approving a new app was not how useful or unique it was, but the amount of battery life it consumed. I watched many a remarkable app get denied because it was going to use too much energy and cripple the ability for the consumer to use their iPhone, iPad, or iPod (remember those?) for a reasonable amount of time. I mean, how mobile is your device if you have to plug it in every twenty minutes to recharge?

Most of the things we do in life drain our spiritual energy rather than restore it. I've never met a person, especially in a work environment, who doesn't know what it's like to be overwhelmed and feel the energy failure and side effects that come with building a business. It can be downright soul-draining at times. So it is imperative that our power source is secure, strong, has a deep reservoir, and ever-charging so that in the times of extreme load we don't crash, collapse, and fail. We have to be sure that the capacity of our spiritual batteries is the best it can be and growing.

This comes through being connected with the power source—it comes through our relationship with our Creator.

Unfortunately, far too many of us are running close to spiritual empty or are not taking the time to internalize the faith code upon which our lives should be based. We are trying to write our own shortcuts and "hacks" into the code to get the love we need and expend as little of it back out

into the world as pos-
sible. If that's how we
live, we're going to run
out of energy. We can't
keep up with the power

> We can't keep up with the power demands of living God's way without staying connected to him as our power source.

demands of living God's way without staying connected to
him as our power source. We just can't do it on our own.

To run our lives well, we have to be "charged up" and
operating according to the Designer's parameters. Humanly,
many of the "code commands" of the Bible can seem con-
tradictory or counterintuitive: Things like *"to be the greatest,
be servant of all,"*[9] *"if anyone slaps you on the right cheek, turn
to him the other also,"*[10] or *"Whoever forces you to go one mile,
go with him two."*[11] We often don't see God's principles as
efficient, let alone effective, but God is not about efficiency
so much as creating the conditions for his love to exist and
thrive. That takes some work and that takes some time,
which is one more reason for keeping our spiritual batteries
well charged at all times.

Operating God's way may take longer, but it's a renewable
energy source. God's systems aren't like cars that run out of
gas and must be refilled (or run out of electricity and have
to be recharged), but like an ecosystem that self-perpetuates.
I think that is how love is supposed to operate—it is the
ultimate self-regenerating power source. God isn't about us
plugging into him for a while and then going out and doing
wonderful things *for* him until we run out of gas (or electricity) and need to be refueled—God wants to establish
his love *with us*, creating cycles of regenerative energy and

increasing capacity wherever we go. That means a continual connection to the Source of all things.

In a recent video entitled "Finding Our Entrepreneurial Identity,"[12] Phil Vischer describes the trap we can fall into by thinking God is pleased with us because we are "doing things *for* him" rather than doing things *with* him. Phil, in case you don't know him, was the creator and producer of VeggieTales, and he was on the way to becoming what he described as "the Christian Walt Disney" before he hit a storm and had to sell VeggieTales to avoid bankruptcy. As Phil had to learn the hard way by losing his dreams and having to start over from scratch, God didn't need a new Walt Disney, he wanted a Phil Vischer. And God didn't want Phil to do things *for* him, he wanted Phil to do things *with* him. That discovery transformed Phil's life.

Phil learned it wasn't about "plugging in" in the morning and then going out into the crazy world to fight for God, hardly ever giving God another thought in the midst of the day, but finding a way to be *with* God continually and try to participate in what *he* was doing, side by side, in step with his Spirit.* As he advises in the video, "Keep your eyes on your Creator. You aren't working for him; you're walking with him. And out of that walk will come the character and the work that will bless the world around you." Walking with him in the dailies is how we keep our capacities growing and overflowing.

God's love and power is never ceasing. We know that. But we must also remember that the capacity of this inner power

---

* Terry note: see Galatians 5:25.

source depends upon just how well we are plugged into him and how well we are living according to the faith code in our daily actions—how consistently we are *hearing* the words of Jesus and *doing* what he asks of us. He is never called "the God of the burned out and used up" anywhere in the Bible—but he is referred to as "the God of abundance" more than once.*

In the scriptures Terry shared, Jesus said we are to love God with our heart, soul, mind, and strength. What if we took a minute each day to see how well we are doing that as a way of checking in on the health of our inner worlds? It might look like a series of questions like these:

Heart	Mind
What are you loving?	What's taking up most of your mental bandwidth?

Soul	Strength
What's feeding your soul? What's eating away at it?	What energizes you? What are you doing to increase your capacities?

God created *us* to be intermediaries between the spiritual world and the created world. We are to live out what it is God has given us to do *imago dei*, "in God's image." When we live in step with our Creator, we find a non-stop source to power our lives, relationships, and missions.

---

* Another Terry note: see Deuteronomy 30:9, 2 Corinthians 9:8, and Philippians 4:19 to start.

More than one person has woken up after twenty years into their careers and wondered how they become the person they are now when their intentions were much different when they started out. (Midlife crisis anyone?) Unless we build and draw on the faith code—the "open source" of

> Unless we build and draw on the faith code—the "open source" of God's Word that helps us walk in the love of God and increases the capacity and strength of our inner being—we're likely to wake up one day to find out we've become someone we never intended to be.

God's Word that helps us walk in the love of God and increases the capacity and strength of our inner being—we're likely to wake up one day to find out we've become someone we never intended to be. (Remember that keyboard-clicking drone sitting next to my wife? I've never liked that guy.) If we're not being formed by God's elegant source code and powered by loving him, chances are our identities are being formed by the external influences around us—and especially the culture of our workplace (at least that's been my experience). That tends to be far from healthy.

Is that who you really want to be? Did God call you to your workplace to conform to it or to transform it with his love?

That is why loving God is the first and highest commandment that Jesus told us to live by. It is the pearl of great price worth everything we own; the treasure in the field worth paying everything we have to obtain.* It is the kingdom he

---

* Terry note: see Matthew 13:44–46.

has asked us to create *with* him—the great adventure he is setting before each and every one of us.

REFLECTION QUESTIONS

1. Before reading this chapter, how would you have defined "love"? What does it mean to you to love God *"with all your heart, with all your soul, with all your mind, and with all your strength"*?

2. Are you better at loving God or loving others? Why? Does loving God help you love others better? How? Why?

3. Read 1 Corinthians 13. Take 5–10 minutes and paraphrase that passage in your own words. What does it say about love you'd never considered before?

4. Are there areas where you already feel God's love? Where don't you? How can you change that?

5. How are you allowing your love for God and your love for others to show up in the different aspects of your life? How often? Are there other ways you'd like to express it in the future?

THREE

THE THREE LOVES

"This is how everyone will recognize that you are my disciples—when they see the love you have for each other."

—*John 13:35* MSG

John chapter 13 begins the story of a remarkable night in the life of Jesus. It is the night of the Last Supper, the night Jesus was betrayed by one of his own, the last night he would spend with his disciples in his life on the earth.

They, though, had no idea of the significance of the evening. In fact, the disciples appeared to be squabbling again about who knows what, once again trying to prove their loyalty to Jesus, which of them should receive the most honor in his coming kingdom, which was the smartest, which would be the best leader, who got to sit next to Jesus at the Passover meal, or whatever—striving with each other to prove themselves the better man; to establish their identities as someone important and worthy of respect.

So what does Jesus do? He doesn't chide them or tell them to stop squabbling. John tells us that instead Jesus *"laid aside his outer garments, and taking a towel, tied it around his waist. Then he poured water into a basin and began to wash the disciples' feet and to wipe them with the towel that was wrapped around him."*[1]

When he was finished, Jesus dressed again, and sat with them. He told them, "Do you understand what I've done? I am your teacher, and you call me 'Lord.' And I am. But I've washed your feet, a task usually saved for the lowliest. This is how you should be treating one another, because you're not greater than me."

And then he went on to say this—the very first lesson in an evening of what would be the most personal teaching of his time on the earth: *"A new commandment I give to you, that you love one another: just as I have loved you, you also are to love one another. By this all people will know that you are my disciples, if you have love for one another."*[2]

He was saying, "This is how people will know that you are plugged into me: *by the love that you exhibit for each other.*"

He could have said a lot of other things here. He could have said the way people will know you are my followers is by your utter devotion, or by how much time you spend studying the scriptures and praying, by being in synagogue every week, by forsaking all and going to the mission field, or even by your willingness to die for me. Or he could have said it was by feeding the poor, or by fighting for justice for the oppressed, or by being a blessing wherever you go, or by doing any number of other "good works" he could have asked them to do as a sign of their allegiance to him.

But he didn't mention any of those things. Instead, he left them with the example of washing their feet and then told them, "People will know you love me through the way you *love one another.*" In this, and through many other examples in his life, he was teaching them to love with their words and through their actions. He was saying, "Our world will know you are my true followers when you love one another as I have loved you."

HOW LOVE SHOWS UP

In the last chapter, Rusty and I proposed that the first of the Great Commandments—*"You shall love the Lord your God with all your heart and with all your soul and with all your mind and with all your strength"*—is the source of how we love others. It is what gives us the capacity and ability to love with God's love so we can do "greater things"[3]—not in our own strength, but with God.

That is the first love we are called to express if we are going to be followers of Jesus.

The second and third love are found in what Jesus said next: *"You shall love your neighbor as yourself."* I think they are together because they set the standard for each other. There is a deep affirmation within this call to love. Buried within this statement is God eternal's declaration of our worth—of the immense value of who he created each of us to be, both inwardly and outwardly.

Why? Because it's hard to do one without the other.

A lot of people struggle loving themselves. No, I know, I totally agree with the "I am third" principle: God is first, others are second, and I am third. But loving others as ourselves has a fundamental requirement: *that we love ourselves in a healthy life-giving way.* It is the foundation of and defines the parameters of how we are to love others. When we see ourselves as "less than," we tend to compete with others for self-worth or let someone else determine our value and make a doormat of ourselves. *Those are* not *love.* But if we know who we are, if we have a solid sense of self-acceptance (even with our imperfections) because we understand how God truly sees us and loves us, that builds a foundation for some exceptional, unselfish, truly unconditional love to others!

I remember someone coming to me after a service once when I was preaching on the Great Commandment and telling me, "I have trouble in all those areas. I feel very bad about myself. I tend to be codependent because I have such a low sense of my own worth." She was so wounded.

I admired her honesty, and I told her so. Then I said, "Let's make it a goal for this next year to get just a little bit better in every area, and that means being able to love ourselves a little better as well. Because, you know what? God loves us, and that makes it okay to love ourselves too."

A lot of our relational issues are connected. When we do not see ourselves properly as a son or daughter of the Lord—when we are not recognizing our true identity in relationship to God—it means we haven't allowed his love to define us, and that affects our capacity to love others. Oftentimes we are so broken on the inside and no one even knows we're struggling. That has a lot to do with how we see ourselves, and that affects our capacity to love. We're struggling to allow Christ's

> When we do not see ourselves properly as a son or daughter of the Lord—when we are not recognizing our true identity in relationship to God—it means we haven't allowed his love to define us, and that affects our capacity to love others.

love for us to be solid ground beneath our feet, but that's what it is. God invites us to see ourselves through the lens of the love he has for us, and then to love others through that lens as well.

When I think of that, the first thing that comes to mind is when another Jewish religious lawyer came to Jesus and asked a question very similar to the one we dealt with in the last chapter. This time the man's motives weren't as pure, but Jesus's response was just as powerful. Luke 10 tells us the lawyer started by asking, *"Teacher, what shall I do to inherit eternal life?"*[4]

Jesus answered the man's question with a question, as he often did. "Well, you're a religious lawyer. What do you think? What is written in the law? How do you interpret it?"

The man answered, "Well, I see it like this: You shall love the Lord your God with all your heart, with all your soul, with all your mind, with all your strength. And the second is like unto it: You should love your neighbor as yourself."

Jesus responds, "You know what? I couldn't have said it better myself. You've answered beautifully. Go and do that."

I don't know if it was because of the way Jesus was—I'm convinced that Jesus had a way of seeing right through people's words to the motives behind them—or if it was in the way he phrased it, but something about Jesus's answer seemed to convict the man.

Luke tells us he answered *"desiring to justify himself."*[5] What Jesus said had put him on the defensive. He seemed to be wondering, "How do I apply that? Where do I draw the line? I mean, come on. It's not that easy. I'm not God. I can't love *everyone*. Who does God mean by 'my neighbor,' anyway? How far does this obligation go?"

Why did he ask this? Because, to the Jewish mind at the time, *neighbor* was limited to "my fellow Jew." (And that's not a Jewish shortcoming—we all do that!) In fact, many taught Jewish people were not responsible to love Gentiles— especially *not* the Romans. There was a lot of cultural tension between the Jewish people and their occupiers, and there has to be a limit, right? So, who *don't* we have to love?

But Jesus replied, "Well, since you asked, let me tell you a story."

"There was a man who went from Jerusalem to Jericho, and he fell among thieves—he got mugged. It was a notoriously dangerous road, he was taking a big risk traveling it alone, and he paid for it. The robbers weren't content just to steal his goods, either. They decided they were going to strip him down and beat him up as well, then they left him on the side of the road to bleed out. That's the picture.

"Now by chance, there was a certain priest who happened by. The priest looked at the man and he passed by on the other side of the road. He didn't want to get involved. He was in a hurry to an important appointment, no doubt. Who knows why he looked the other way, but that's what he did.

"After that a Levite, someone who worked in the temple and was a member of God's consecrated tribe, came and did basically the same thing. He came, he looked a little bit closer, but he also decided it best not to take a chance. Maybe he thought it was a trap. There was a legitimate fear of that. He'd heard of it happening to others.

"Better to not get involved. *Sorry.*

"Then a third man came by, and this man was a Samaritan."

It's interesting that Jesus chose to make the hero of his story a Samaritan, because there were ethnic, racial, and religious tensions between Samaritans and the Jewish people. Samaritans were half Jewish, and they had their own kind of hybrid expression of Judaism. It would be an understatement to say this was racial tension as well. Neither liked the other much, and they tried to avoid each other as much as they could with their own version of segregation. If possible, they would go all the way around the other's territory just to avoid possibly running into someone from the other group.

The crowd listening would have instantly had the hair on the back of their necks stand up at the mention of this person. They had deep prejudices against Samaritans.

After what I imagine as a pause to let that point sink in, Jesus continued, "The Samaritan saw the man and felt compassion for him. He went to him, treated and bandaged his wounds, covered him, and put him on his donkey to take him to the next available town.

"Upon arrival, he rented the man a room in an inn so that he would have a bed where he could rest and recover. The next day, when the Samaritan was leaving, he took out two denarii (which was a considerable sum of money—two full days of wages, scholars tell us), and he told the innkeeper,

'I've got to go, but take care of this man until I get back. Whatever more you spend, I will repay you upon my return.'

"So," Jesus then asked, "which of these three do you think was a 'neighbor' to the man who fell among the thieves and was left for dead?"

I imagine the lawyer answered rather sheepishly, "The one who showed mercy."

"You go and do likewise," Jesus concluded.

In Jesus's story, the Samaritan won the day because he acted in love toward the person in need next to him. Obedience to the Great Commandment wasn't believing a certain way, belonging to a specific tribe, ethnicity, or group, or being in a holy occupation. It was seeing someone in need and acting to help—*to love* that person. Jesus was saying it's not enough to talk about love and never help others, never to love strangers—or never to love an "enemy."

In short, Jesus transformed the question "Who is my neighbor?" into "Will you be a neighbor?" Will you feel a tug on your heart for a person or a people group you just happen across while you are walking through life minding your own business? That may be God prompting you

> Jesus transformed the question "Who is my neighbor?" into "Will you be a neighbor?"

to love them. That is what Jesus is asking us to do. Love is not abstract; it is expressed through words and actions.

Part of what the Lord is getting at here, I think, is that we'll never know the joy of loving others unless we learn that it is more blessed to give than it is to receive. The truly blessed, happy life is filled with love that takes action whenever it sees a neighbor in need, even if it forces us out of our comfort zone (and maybe especially if it does!).

So, let me ask you: *Just how are the three loves of God showing up in your life?*

"HACKING" LOVE

Great job, Terry, in laying out what Jesus taught about loving God, ourselves, and our neighbors. Jesus made it very clear: The Samaritan got it right and the priest and the Levite did not, no matter what their standing was in their society. As we walk out of the Word and into our daily lives, it is critical that we work hard to "live out" loving in word and deed, just as Jesus prescribed.

But that gives me pause. As a tech leader and entrepreneur at heart, it gets my mind churning. In my space, we like to take ideas and see if there is a way to use them to innovate. We like to take new technology convergences and see if we can disrupt an industry, turning it upside down, so to speak, and creating something completely new that helps people in transformational ways, like the Model T did to horse and buggies, airplanes did to trains, digital cameras in our phones did to Kodak, Facebook did to MySpace, and Netflix did to Blockbuster, and soon ChatGPT and other large neural networks will do to everything we thought we knew about how to interact with technology and knowledge bases.

In Jesus's time, I think it is clear he meant the love of God he was talking about was to disrupt culture and turn religious traditions back upside right. He was breathing life into their dry interpretations of the Law of Moses and showing the power of transformed hearts vs. religious stringency. As Terry described it in chapter one, Jesus started by preaching "You have heard it said . . . but I say to you . . . ." He came so that Israel—and eventually the world—would see the representation of his Father living, breathing, and operating among them.

In essence, love disrupts a status quo. Jesus came to introduce his own "Netflix"—the love of God—to overturn the "Blockbuster" of traditions and wrong interpretations that had developed over the centuries. He was restoring original principles, eliminating bureaucracy, and creating a "straight to the consumer" connection to God. In many ways, Jesus was the ultimate cultural innovator.

> Love disrupts a status quo. Jesus came to introduce his own "Netflix"—the love of God—to overturn the "Blockbuster" of traditions and wrong interpretations that had developed over the centuries.

In Silicon Valley it is often said we "hack" a technology or concept when we use it to make it better, or serve different functions, and disrupt the way a marketplace operated before. In a negative sense, that means taking something and seeing how to break it, but that's rarely the meaning used by entrepreneurs. Instead, "hacking" is about actualizing an idea or technology in a way that replaces the old with something far more effective. It often makes a longer process obsolete or introduces a completely new way to meet a need, address an issue, or solve a problem. It can even leapfrog technologies, as cell phones have done to landlines in

Africa and elsewhere. This has allowed them to bypass using cash for commerce with digital transfers, accessing banking without ever seeing a teller or even needing a bank in their town, accessing information without printed newspapers or a radio, connecting with distant friends and relatives, and so much more. Even people still living in mud huts—without electricity—have cell phones today (charging them at a local store or bar).

But an idea is not enough. Companies with great, innovative ideas fail every day, and often sell to someone who can be successful with it where they couldn't. What that someone else has that the inventor didn't is a stable system for bringing the product to market and building a business around it, even a completely new industry, if necessary. They are the ones who successfully "hack"—operationalize or actualize—the idea into something that brings immense change. Maybe even an idea that could "save the world." That was Jesus's plan, anyway—and he aimed to do it with the love of God.

I think we have fallen short with this in similar ways to the religious leaders of Jesus's time, because of a severe lack of imagination. First, we have not understood the true nature of love. Second, we haven't built it into our lives and cultures in systematic ways that will disrupt the way the world around us does things. We have to a point, of course, and there have been incredible transformations in the past, but I think God is calling us to new "parting the Red Sea"-sized things today. I think God wants us to take his love global in ways that have never been done before. He wants us to take the "Good News" of Jesus into every realm of life, not just the religious. He also wants us to take it into business, media, government, education, arts and entertainment, neighborhoods, friend groups, and family.[6] He wants it to transform every area of life and change the way the world operates. He wants us to create rather than extract, plug into his abundance rather than be limited by lack, take responsibility rather than point fingers, empower rather than exploit, and to steward our world into regeneration rather than strip it to the bone and burn up its resources.

In fact, you can remember those things with an acronym: **CARES**—because love **CARES**. The love of God:

Creates new things and ways (makes something out of virtually nothing, if you will—like a new idea or way of doing things),
Operates in **Abundance** (as opposed to being extractive or exploitive),
takes and inspires **Responsibility**,
Empowers individuals and people groups,
and **Stewards** what God has entrusted to us.

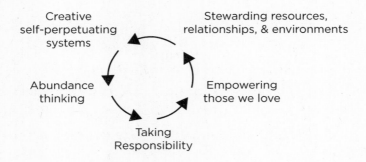

I think it's good to evaluate anything we do with those five concepts to see if it is truly love or not, whether it is an action, a ministry, a cause, a policy, a law, a program, or a business. Just how does any action we take, whether in the moment or premeditated, reflect loving God, loving ourselves, and loving others? It should become a regenerative cycle.

In his book, *If Aristotle Ran General Motors*, Tom Morris, chairman of the Morris Institute of Human Values, said it this way: "The meaning of life is creative love. Not love as an inner feeling, as a private sentimental emotion, but love as a dynamic power moving out into the world and doing something original."[7]

We are *commanded* to love, after all, but every letter of God's Word inspires it as well. Love is what reflects the nature of heaven to the world around us. It is what St. Augustine called creating "the City of God," what Martin Luther termed filling our communities with "common grace"—so instilling love into our daily lives that it would permeate our offices, agencies, and mission statements. It brings heaven to earth for all of society to experience. It is what Jesus meant by the kingdom of God. It's taking God's goodness into every aspect of life and letting the way we serve one another reflect his glory.

I have spent a bunch of time with companies and organizations in the development of their purpose (Why?), mission (What?), and values (How?) statements, and I can't wait until I find the company that has the desire and courage to explicitly state that one of their core principles is loving people.

Entrepreneurs take an idea and build a—hopefully—self-regenerating system around it, so that it fills a need and produces cash while doing it, so that it can pay salaries and keep the lights on. Entrepreneurs wonder how they can create systems that will preemptively meet needs, solve problems, and address issues. Then they spin that system into action and let it transform cultures and industries.

I'm not talking about some kind of unattainable utopia, but our generation and the next ones coming up will have access to resources and possibilities never before seen. While many fear technology for how it is changing us and often disconnecting us from one another, that is because we are not being as mindful as we should be in how we are using it. Most definitely, technology and systems can be "weaponized" so that we win at the expense of everyone else. We see that happen all the time. But that is because they are being used outside of the love of God and with the love of God outside of their thinking. What if, instead, we made implementing the love of God the hub of our creative thought life and the organizations we form as entrepreneurs?

We live in a world where there is a lot of pain and a powerful temptation to turn our eyes away from the biggest and most challenging problems and live in a smaller, separate, protected world. But more than ever in history, I believe that's no longer possible. When a flood hits India, we hear about it within the hour. The same with an earthquake

> What if, instead, we made implementing the love of God the hub of our creative thought life and the organizations we form as entrepreneurs?

that hits Japan, Turkey, or Syria, or when a volcano erupts in South America. When Russia attacked Ukraine, we should have realized that there are no more wars that aren't world wars—the ripples and ramifications have been felt everywhere. We are the generation that can't stick our heads in the sand. Every time we hear about one of these things, it asks, "So, what are you going to do to help? How is the love of God going to show up in this situation?"

I don't believe there is anything that we can do through human willpower or political systems alone. Help to those in need and transformation to solve chronic problems will demand good, innovative people in the right places doing the right things from the right motivations. And I don't believe that will come about without the love of God being the primary driver.

Jesus is calling us to create, to think abundantly, to take responsibility, to empower, and to steward well when he tells us to live by God's love. After all, he is our example and said so himself: *"just as I have loved you, you also are to love one another."*[8]

That is the right foundation to build a life on: loving God, to continually be increasing our spiritual capacity and energizing our minds and souls, loving ourselves in a healthy way, and then acting out God-inspired ideas for the betterment of all around us. If we want the complete suite, that is faith code framework: Applying God's love (you might even say, through

> If we want the complete suite, that is faith code framework: Applying God's love in a life of faith that is running at full and abundant capacity from the love of God we are experiencing ourselves.

applications or "apps") in a life of faith that is running at full and abundant capacity from the love of God we are experiencing ourselves. That's the adventure of letting God's love power every application—"app"—of God's Word, of his "faith code." That's living like the Good Samaritan on the grandest of scale.

And that's the life I'm after.

You in?

REFLECTION QUESTIONS

1. How are the three loves showing up in your life? Where could you use more of the love of God channeling through you?

2. Read Luke 10:25–37. What does this story say to you personally? Given this context: who is the neighbor that needs you the most right now?

3. Consider the five mindsets of love again that Rusty proposed: creativity, abundance, responsibility, empowerment, and stewardship (**CARES**). How do you see these mindsets being expressed in your day-to-day life? Where could you use more of them?

4. What is a time someone loved you in a way that really touched your life? How do you express gratitude for that in the way you love others?

5. How do you develop your capacity for loving in each of the key roles of your life? (As a son or daughter of God, as a family member, in your work, and as part of a church community, etc.?)

PART II

BUILDING THE FRAMEWORK

"Therefore I tell you, do not be anxious about your life, what you will eat or what you will drink, nor about your body, what you will put on. Is not life more than food, and the body more than clothing? . . . For the Gentiles seek after all these things, and your heavenly Father knows that you need them all. But seek first the kingdom of God and his righteousness, and all these things will be added to you."

—*Matthew 6:25, 32–33*

FOUR

THE GROWTH IMPERATIVE

> "How can I describe the Kingdom of God? What story should I use to illustrate it? It is like a mustard seed planted in the ground. It is the smallest of all seeds, but it becomes the largest of all garden plants; it grows long branches, and birds can make nests in its shade."
>
> —*Mark 4:30-32* NLT

It is one of the most intriguing scenes in the Gospels. People loved to see and hear Jesus. As Jesus was teaching on the seaside one day, the crowd grew so large that they began to push him into the surf. In response, Jesus showed his ingenuity and compassion. Rather than moving to another location or cancelling the teaching to "keep the Master dry," he stepped into a boat and pushed out from the shore. Once he could again lock eyes with each member in his audience, he taught from there. As I (Terry) imagine it, I see the people, sitting on the beach in a sort of natural amphitheater, Jesus's voice booming off the water for all to hear.

Jesus told a series of parables that day, including what he described as a keystone to all parables—*"Do you not understand this parable? How then will you understand all the parables?"*[1]—the Parable of the Sower.[2]

Along with this, however, is one of his lesser-known parables, overlooked, perhaps, because of its auspicious neighbor. The parable of the growing seed is often read past without much reflection. I feel it's worth more attention though and has some valuable lessons. It unlocks its own principles about the nature of God's kingdom that we should all keep at the forefront of our minds.

The kingdom of God is as if a man should scatter seed on the ground. He sleeps and rises night and day, and the seed sprouts and grows; he knows not how. The earth produces by itself, first the blade, then the ear, then the full grain in the ear. But when the grain is ripe, at once he puts in the sickle, because the harvest has come.[3]

Many are fascinated by Jesus for the miracles and healings he performed, and with good reason. But in this central passage of his teaching, he repeatedly likens all he brings to teach people in his sermons—in his words—not to hearty, full-grown plants, but to *seeds*. Here, he likens the kingdom of God to a man sleeping and rising, day in and day out, to grow a crop starting with those smallest of all things.

What is it in this growing cycle that he wants us to understand? Why is growth such a consistent theme in his teachings? How are we to understand that our missions on the earth are like this farmer raising a crop?

Let's dig into the parable a bit more and see what we can discover.

FAITH AND PATIENCE

Like so many of the parables Jesus told, he set it in the world of the commonplace. He speaks of a farmer and the growing cycle—seedtime and harvest—something everyone in his audience would understand.

The farmer does the planting. He scatters the seed and then he begins to wait. *"He sleeps and rises night and day"*[4] for several weeks. And then something happens. *"And the seed sprouts and grows; he knows not how."*[5] It's a miracle, of sorts, though as natural as the turning of the seasons. After a certain time, the seed sprouts underground and begins reaching down in the soil for nutrients and up toward the sun for light. There's kind of a mystery to what happens under the surface: *"The earth produces by itself."*[6] Then, after a time, the farmer sees the results of the seed sown and it bears fruit: *"first the blade, then the ear, then the full grain in the ear."*[7] There's a melody to it—a rhythm. *"But when the grain is ripe, at once he puts in the sickle, because the harvest has come."*[8] What he planted all those months before is now producing a blessing that will benefit many.

This entire passage is about the power of the "seeds" we sow. In explaining the nearby Parable of the Sower, Jesus tells his disciples, *"The sower sows the word."*[9] I believe we sow seeds with our words and also with our actions. Jesus is telling us what we say and do matters, as do the intentions behind those words and deeds.

Intentions are the potential in the seeds sown—don't underestimate their power. They are like the life force that turns an acorn into a mighty oak tree, or a mustard seed into something birds of the air can build their nests in. Like seeds, words and deeds are scattered and will bring forth after their kind. This process cannot be stopped without pulling up the newborn plant and potentially wasting the seed.

You know, I think it's quite common to underestimate the power of our thoughts, words, and actions over time, much less the potency of the intentions behind them. Jesus likens them to seeds for a reason—at the beginning, they are small and seem insignificant; over time, however, they will grow into something substantial and will affect the lives and livelihoods of others. He likens it to creating a society—the kingdom of God. Our words and actions will have a ripple effect, like a stone thrown into still waters.

When we speak a kind word to a coworker and get a sharp reply, we think that means it has had no effect, but if we continue to speak to them kindly over time, they will eventually see us as someone who they can trust. Even something as little as showing up on time for meetings or texting someone to know you will be delayed when things got away from you will have a cumulative effect. If such little things can matter, how much more can our attitudes conveyed in our words and actions? There is tremendous power in daily loving words and actions, just as there is tremendous power in unloving words and actions over time. Far too many of us know the effects of those, and many of us carry trauma from them.

In any and every area of our lives, we will not be the same people in ten years that we are today. Sure, some things will look similar, but we will grow or decay depending on what we sow into our souls and the souls of others. It's easy to think we don't matter or that we'll never amount to much, but that's like evaluating people at the start rather than the finish line of a race—the difference is determined by how the race in the middle is run, not by where you are at the beginning.

A word spoken in love is a seed of love, and a word spoken in anger is a seed of anger—sow enough of either kind and they have a cumulative effect. Jesus teaches here that a seed, once planted, is a dynamic, unwearying, unstoppable force that— even when we waver and are in need of rest or replenishment—grows in

> A word spoken in love is a seed of love, and a word spoken in anger is a seed of anger—sow enough of either kind and they have a cumulative effect.

ways seen and unseen. The power in the seed can never be fully appreciated nor understood until the time of harvest. The life we build comes from the seeds we sow.

In Ecclesiastes, Solomon wrote: *"God has made everything beautiful for its own time. He has planted eternity in the human heart, but even so, people cannot see the whole scope of God's work from beginning to end."*[10] There is a part of us that longs for more, longs to live, and longs to know our place in the big picture of the universe—to release the eternity in our hearts—but all we ever have to work with is the present. In the parable of the growing seed, Jesus reminds us that there are principles of growth that pertain to living a flourishing life—principles of growth we should be listening for and pursuing—and we sow them one word or action at a time.

It all goes back, once again, to the Great Commandment: *"You shall love the Lord your God with all your heart and with all your soul and with all your mind and with all your strength."*[11] Let's take a deeper look at those four parts of our being—heart, soul, mind, and strength—and talk a bit more of how we can nurture our capacity in each of these realms each and every day.

"Love the Lord with all of your heart."

Again, what do you love? And just as importantly, how are you loving them?

Don't answer too quickly. It's odd that we are so quick to say *what* we love (and dilute the word—like, "I love my new car"), but not quick to explain *why* and *how* that love emanates in our lives. We often "love" things not for themselves, but because they do something *for us*. A new car, for example, gives us status, makes us feel a certain way, energizes us when we drive it, or any of a number of things like that. A lot of times, it tends to be more about us than whoever or whatever we are loving.

When we love God—when we really love him—are we steadfast or fickle? Is it all about what God can do for us? Is it all about blessings and promises? Don't get me wrong, those are wonderful and shouldn't be denied, but when we hit a storm, is our first thought "Where is God in this? Why has he forsaken me?" or do we turn to him and say something along the lines of, "Okay, that happened, what do *we* do now, Lord?"

I've always found that's when following Jesus really begins.

"Love the Lord with all of your soul."

So, how are you? How is your *soul*? How is your internal well-being?

When is the last time you considered that question *honestly* and you didn't just blurt out "I'm fine" or "doing great"?

Perhaps it's time to reconsider our pat responses.

Now I don't mean that we have to take every casual greeting of "How are you?" as an opportunity for a counseling session, but at least once a day, we need to consider the state of our souls more seriously because the capacity and condition of our souls drive a great deal of our lives. Are we quick to anger when someone makes a mistake, or we think we were belittled in some way? When our identities are fragile, we don't ooze with the fruit of the Spirit[12]—love, joy, peace, patience, kindness, goodness, faithfulness, gentleness, self-control— but the works of the flesh[13]—manipulation, ill will, strife, jealousy, rivalries, dissensions, and division, to name a few.

It is hard to love properly from a wounded or insecure soul.

"Love the Lord with all of your mind."

So, how is your thought life? What do you spend most of your time thinking about? Is God part of those inner conversations?

Our minds often seem so chaotic. We certainly all have random thoughts that we wouldn't want others to hear or

71

see. I don't really know if there is a way to prevent such things, but I don't think they define us either. What I think does define us is what we choose to think about, mull over, and dwell on for extended periods of time. What do you *choose* to think about on a regular basis?

All that we create in this world starts in our minds. All that we input, learn, all that we understand, all that we are able to successfully apply, all begin in our thoughts and attitudes, in the intellectual domain. Many have said "Necessity is the mother of invention," but I don't think that's exactly right. If anything, necessity is the father of invention, imagination is what nurtures it in its womb and gives it birth.

So just how are you loving God in your thoughts and with your mind?

"Love the Lord with all of your strength."

Are you healthy in spirit, soul, and body? Are you resilient, or do the littlest things rock your boat?

Certainly, it is good to be strong in body, but strengths are also emotional and important to our character. Do things people say rattle you easily? Can you work on something for eight hours in the day and not feel the need to binge out on something unhealthy to compensate? How are your habits? Your self-discipline? What do you do for recreation and how does it nurture and rejuvenate you?

Each of these parts of who we are—heart, soul, mind, and strength—are internal elements that contribute to forming our identities. They are the building blocks of our inner selves and the battery cells that power our external actions. They underpin our attitudes, confidences, convictions, mindsets, emotions, personality, determination, dreams and aspirations, likes, skills and talents, capacities, and all the things that go into making us *us*. They make up our inner world, a world that is either plugged into the framework and influences the world around us, or the part of us that tries to conform to the world so that we can feel accepted and appreciated. These are two very different approaches to how we show up in the world, and one is indeed building on something rock solid, while the other is constructing on shifting sands.

Lasting good takes time to create. The predominant law of God's kingdom is gradual growth through one good endeavor at a time. It demands faith and patience, for it is through "*faith and patience* [we] *inherit the promises.*"[14]

> The predominant law of God's kingdom is gradual growth through one good endeavor at a time. It demands faith and patience.

God is developmental. Most of what he does is not cataclysmic, but gradual. First Corinthians 13:13 tells us that the three things that will endure forever are "*faith, hope, and love*"—love being the greatest of the three. This means we need to be people who remain optimistic and hopeful, celebrating every victory, always grateful, encouraging, and confident of the growth of the words and deeds of love we sow into the lives of others.

AN APP FOR THIS:
GROW OR . . . ?

Terry is particularly fond of one statement that has become very relevant in the past years: "If you are going to go through it, you might as well grow through it." It's a challenge we should all take up.

Organisms either grow or die. The same can be said of organizations (perhaps why they are both adapted from the same word). There is no standing still and remaining the same. Marketing guru Seth Godin put it this way, "An organism constantly changes. The cells develop, die, and are replaced. It adapts to the current environment or goes away." Yep, that could be in a company, nonprofit, institution, agency, or home—wherever we tend to spend the bulk of our waking energies and hours.

At the same time, we seem to forget that all these very complex, sometimes massive, organizations are made up of organisms called people, and we (those organisms) *must* also grow, or we (literally or figuratively) die as well. Like a tree reaching toward the sky, we're all on a journey on this earth that only ends when we die. Everything we face, success or setback, is just part of that journey. As Orson Welles once wrote, "If you want a happy ending, that depends, of course, on where you stop your story." Whether an incident in our lives is a challenge or a deal-breaker—something to overcome toward a larger goal or a defeat—is all a matter of which part of our story it is, and whether we let it define who we are ("I'm a failure") or see it as an opportunity to grow and have a more victorious outcome down the road ("I'm just not where I want to be yet").

Stanford professor and author Carol Dweck wrote about these two perspectives in her book, *Mindset: The New Psychology of Success*. In her own words, she identifies that we all tend to have either a "fixed" or a "growth" mindset. In a very real way, those with a fixed mindset see every challenge as a test of all they will ever be capable of accomplishing. Why? Because, deep down, they believe their intelligence, talents, athletic ability, or their capabilities in general are "fixed." Thus every failure reminds them that they don't have what it takes. They are plagued with a fear that they will never be enough to accomplish their dreams and aspirations. They don't have setbacks, they have stop signs. Each unmet challenge is a blow to their identity—a reminder that they just don't measure up. As Dweck describes it:

> Believing that your qualities are carved in stone—the fixed mindset—creates an urgency to prove yourself over and over. If you have only a certain amount of intelligence, a certain personality, and a certain moral character—well, then you'd better prove that you have a healthy dose of them.[15]

A person with a growth mindset evaluates the same "failures" quite differently, however. Their analysis is more along the lines of, "Okay, not there yet. I need to reevaluate and do something different before I face a challenge like this again." It's not a slight to their ego or personhood, but, as Henry Ford once said, "Failure is simply the opportunity to begin again, this time more intelligently." Like a Thomas Edison, they don't get sidetracked by experiments that don't work, they just see them as one more thing that isn't the right answer yet. They're on a journey somewhere and each failure is just a step closer to it.

While those with a fixed mindset tend to want to "have arrived," growth mindset folks are all about the journey. As Dr. Dweck describes it, a growth mindset

> is based on the belief that your basic qualities are things you can cultivate through your efforts, your strategies, and help from others. Although people may differ in every which way—in their initial talents and aptitudes, interests, or temperaments—everyone can change and grow through application and experience.[16]

To love as God has called us to love, it's really better to have a growth mindset than a fixed one. If we have our identities founded in the fact that God loves us and considers us a member of his family, then what happens around us is just part of the adventure of growing in him, not something that defines all we are capable of. We may be small in some aspect of life at the moment, but we are going to get bigger. We are going to grow. The capacities for what we are capable of are going to increase. It all really depends, again, on what we love and how we love it.

> If we have our identities founded in the fact that God loves us and considers us a member of his family, then what happens around us is just part of the adventure of growing in him, not something that defines all we are capable of.

For me, I like to keep track of this growth in four different areas. When I look into each, they tell me how I am at the moment, what I am loving, and where I should be growing. I call them the four capacity tests. The first is my calendar, the second is my wallet, the third is my words, and the fourth follows closely behind—what am I doing with the authority entrusted to me?

Of all the things we have on this earth, there is nothing more precious than time. Be you a president or a pauper, you have the same number of hours in a day, a week, a month, and a year. Where you spend your time is one of the best ways of telling what really matters to you and whether you are working on growth or struggling to measure up to someone else's expectations.

As I shared in the first chapter, God called me to be in business and he called me to be a good husband, and one cannot replace the other. While of the two, being a good husband to my one wife is the priority, God hasn't called me to that alone. I need to spend time on each, and that time will change, depending on circumstances. I also need to spend time on my relationship with God (which is also beneficial to my time spent at work and with my wife) as well as exercising, learning, and even just relaxing and having some fun.

The degree to which I spend my time appropriately in every area that matters to me determines a great deal. As I learned when I spent my time with my wife on my work instead, things can get out of balance very quickly. (We'll talk more about creating the right rhythm between the things that you love in the next chapter.)

The same could be said for your money. Look at your credit card statement or whatever tool you use to keep track of your finances. Where is your money going? Are you giving? Are you generous? Are you investing in things that are going to make the world a better place? Or is your money going to self-medicating things? Is the recreation you pay for, even in $0.99 bites, helping you become the person God wants you to become or merely anesthetizing you against your pain and fears of inadequacy? Is your identity wrapped up in how much money you make, or is it a tool you're using to take care of your loved ones and make the world a better place? It's certainly worth taking some time to look at what you do with your money and see if it aligns with the purpose and meaning you are pursuing in life.

What do the words that come out of your mouth tell you about the condition of your soul? What are they filled with? Love? Contempt? Anger? Encouragement? Sarcasm? Are they patronizing? Are they edifying? What exactly do your words convey?

> **What do the words that come out of your mouth tell you about the condition of your soul?**

Another thing to consider is what you do with the authority that has been entrusted to you. Is it all about privilege or about service? Do you prioritize "getting things done" or "growing people along the way"? Are people a bother, a help, or a project? What we do with authority is perhaps one of the greatest tests of our character, as fellow politician Robert G. Ingersoll said of Abraham Lincoln:

Nothing discloses real character like the use of power. It is easy for the weak to be gentle. Most people can bear adversity. But if you wish to know what a man really is, give him power. This is the supreme test. It is the glory of Lincoln that, having almost absolute power, he never abused it, except on the side of mercy.[17]

There are more spiritual capacity tests, but I can't think of four more telling metrics than what we do with our time, money, words, and the authority entrusted to us, whether it is at work or organizing a church bake sale. When the chips are down and a storm of life is roaring in your ears, how do you respond? With kindness, humility, justice, power, and equity? If not, it's time to grow.

We choose to run our lives on the faith code so we can have a foundation that is strong, stable, reliable, and lasting. As I thought about what this might look like, the following chart came to mind (I like charts—they help me see relationships and how things influence each other):

Growing Our Capacities

Your identity is formed in the crucible between
your internal and external worlds;
you have the choice to be proactive or
reactive in forming who you show up as

Loving God with:

**Loving ourselves
and others through:**

Heart
What do you love?
And how are you
loving it?

Soul
What's feeding your
soul? What's eating
away at it?

Mind
What's taking up most
of your mental
bandwidth?

Strength
What energizes you?
What are you doing to
increase your various
"fitnesses"?

Identity
Capacity tests

Time

Words   Money

Authority

Growth tests

Realms of life

Re-
creation

Relation-
ships   Vocation

Health

Growth

Rhythm

Intention/
vision

Innovation/
Creativity

Humble in
Success

Resilient in
Failure

Grace/
Forgiveness

Joy

Commitment/
Perseverance

Loving God strengthens our inner self; it is what allows us to grow. We should regularly ask ourselves questions about the health of our heart, soul, mind, and strength. We need to dig into the faith code and define our identities according to how God sees us, not standards external messaging tries to impose on us. We need to become who God has called us to be on the inside so that it empowers our actions on the outside. This develops our capacities and shows up most notably in the areas of our recreation (what we do to refresh and *re*-create ourselves), vocation, relationships, and health (physical, mental, and spiritual "fitnesses").

Love shows up best when we are tuned for growth—when we recognize that our best is always ahead of us, not behind us, as well as the best of others. To do that, we should create a rhythm or routine that will keep us mindful of what we value and that we practice the priorities we espouse. This will allow us to watch for what God is up to, and hopefully plug meaningfully into the purposes he has called us to live out.

We should always be looking to grow in our loves, in our capacities, in our mission, and in our influence for good. It's easy to hold back, but I don't think that is the abundant life Jesus is calling us to. It means being mindful, writing down our goals, exercising godly attitudes, and walking in step with God, guided by his Spirit, throughout all our days.

It's not easy, but I can tell you, from the few times I've felt I've gotten it right, it's so worth it.

REFLECTION QUESTIONS

1. What are areas of your life where you're proudest of your growth in recent years? What are areas where you'd like to see more growth in the coming months?

2. Read Mark 4:1–33. Consider what Jesus is saying about seeds and what becomes of them in these parables. How does what he is saying here apply to you?

3. After reading this passage, why do you think growth is a fundamental principle of the kingdom Jesus was founding? What verses stand out to you? Why?

4. Think of the most significant challenges you have faced in the last year. Have you approached them with a fixed or a growth mindset? What does having a growth mindset make you want to do differently in the future?

5. Which of the four areas—heart, soul, mind, strength—do you feel you need to grow in the most? How would you answer the question each demands of us?

   ° What do you love? And how are you loving it?
   ° What's feeding your soul? What's eating away at it?
   ° What's taking up most of your mental bandwidth?
   ° What energizes you?
   ° What are you doing to increase your various "fitnesses"?

   (Take each one separately and outline some growth activities you should do to increase the health of each one.)

FIVE

LIVING IN A RHYTHM OF GRACE

"Are you tired? Worn out? Burned out on religion? Come to me. Get away with me and you'll recover your life. I'll show you how to take a real rest. Walk with me and work with me—watch how I do it. Learn the unforced rhythms of grace. I won't lay anything heavy or ill-fitting on you. Keep company with me and you'll learn to live freely and lightly."

—*Matthew 11:28–30* MSG

When wondering about original intents, it's often good to go back to the very beginning.

As the first chapter of Genesis tells it, on the first day of the first week—what we now refer to as the week of creation—God set about the task of turning chaos into order and continued to make incremental improvements to that for the next five days. On the sixth day, he finished with his best: creating human beings—a man and a woman fashioned after his own image—and placed them in the midst of all he had already created. The other days had all been good—this sixth day God proclaimed, "very good." (It was the first Friday, after all.)

Then, on the seventh day, he and his creation rested, reflecting on what God had accomplished in the previous six days. He wanted to mark the moment. The Master Artist paused and rested from his work to appreciate the beauty of what his mind and hands had wrought. Not unlike the painter who steps back to view the painting as a whole, God surveyed the goodness of what he had brought to life. It was a masterpiece of unparalleled complexity—vast, grand, and uniquely satisfying. He took a day for reflection and joyful contemplation to simultaneously consider the past but also what he wanted the future to hold.

While the fall of Adam and Eve messed these plans up, it did not change the original pattern. If anything, part of what Jesus came for was to restore that pattern, to teach us how to walk in his Father's *"rhythms of grace."*

"GIVE US THIS DAY . . ."

Each of us (Rusty and I included) needs to find a way to "be" so that we produce "good work" and do work that is "good for us"—something we can sink into wholeheartedly. This kind of "being" is something we accomplish in the routine of our days and of our weeks: time for work, home, recreation, and restoration—time to feed our hearts, minds, and souls as well as fulfill the obligations that are all around us. But it starts with returning to the strength of what we are building our life frameworks on and how we are choosing to engage with the faith code.

In each of the Gospel accounts, if we look closely, we can see how Jesus did just this as he taught and modeled how to live a vital and fruitful life. We are told in Mark, for instance,

> *Rising very early in the morning, while it was still dark, he [Jesus] departed and went out to a desolate place, and there he prayed. And Simon and those who were with him searched for him, and they found him and said to him, "Everyone is looking for you."*[1]

Apparently, it wasn't uncommon for the disciples to wake up and have to go looking for Jesus, not knowing where he had chosen to spend time with his Father that morning. We see, here and there throughout the Gospels, that this was his routine. When he taught his disciples to pray, the words he gave them centered around the phrase, *"give us this day"*[2] emphasizing the importance of prayer as part of one's daily rhythm. Jesus certainly practiced this.

By inference from such passages, we also learn that Jesus was an early riser. He knew early morning is a special time of opportunity. Everything is usually a little easier, mellower, and less stressful, primarily because many are still asleep. (The same could be said late in the evening.)

Jesus did not rise early to "seize the day" and get an early jump on his work, however. He practiced alone time. He went to a "*desolate* [solitary] *place*." He rose early in the morning to be by himself with his Father and his thoughts, not telling anyone where he was going so that it would be less likely he'd be interrupted. Before he engaged his disciples or the crowds or moved into the day, he carved out space apart from others to reflect and be in prayer.

If there was ever anyone who walked on this earth for whom prayer might seem unnecessary, you would think it would be Jesus. But he modeled precisely the opposite. He did not live an independent life, but a dependent one—and he is the blueprint for life lived at its fullest. It appears he viewed his prayer time as a place of essential communication—a source of vital connection with his Father in heaven and learning and implementing his Father's will for the earth.

Prayer and reflection are ways to center ourselves in the priorities and "loves" God has called us to. Jesus ensured prayer and reflection were part of his daily life and part of his weekend rest. Taking time for each of these allows us to clarify who we truly are as members of God's family and his representatives on the earth. It is a way of pushing beyond the noise of the world around us and its constant expectations. Silence allows us to hear what God wants us to know about who we are, who he is calling us to be, and who he wants us to become. It is one of the primary ways to love him.

When we step apart to spend time in silence or conversation with God, we are assured that we are loved just as we are, but also called to be something more. When we know who we are, or at least who we are supposed to be, we can better resist the siren call of those things that are unworthy, unhealthy, and ultimately unfulfilling, which helps us stay grounded in what really matters, no matter what is going on around us. Saying "no" is always easier when we are committed to a bigger "yes."

> Saying "no" is always easier when we are committed to a bigger "yes."

Once we have a sense of vocation and calling in our lives, it's essential that we commit to living it out on a daily and weekly basis, even though we may not know the final destination we will reach twenty or forty years or even sixty years down the road. Clarifying our "first things" or priorities, as foundational as that is, is not enough. For first things to have effect, they have to be lived out in the everydayness of our lives. On many levels, that is exactly what it means to actively love, and that's where really good time management makes the difference. It's the connection that must be made between aspirations and the mundane. It's where the doing takes place. As management guru Stephen Covey used to say, "To learn and not to *do* is really not to learn. To know and not to *do* is really not to know."[3]

The assumption here is that most of us truly want to be better at living out our values and priorities. We want a growing and fulfilling life. We want to squeeze meaning out of our days. When that is our desire, we will inevitably be moved to use our time more intentionally.

I'm convinced all of us should live with humility when it comes to the length of our days and the span of our lives. None of us knows for sure how long we are going to live.

What we can discern with better accuracy is the present season we are in. I suppose many of us will be able to discern a season's twilight when it's coming and start to prepare for the new dawn that will follow. But between now and then we have a great opportunity to live well and wisely on this side of eternity. I believe it's helpful to remind ourselves of a few things:

- Just as with Jesus, the Father has a plan for our lives. There are tasks to accomplish, lives to touch, love to give, service to render, and a contribution to make. There is a great deal of free will in how we do those things—what should our daily rhythm look like so we can stay in the midst of God's plans for us?
- Will we be faithful to think about and reflect upon these "holy" assignments? And then, like Jesus, when they are clear, how will we pursue them, honor them, and seek to live them out in the dailiness of our lives?

There is a need to be both organized and simultaneously nimble in our life approach, primarily because there are going to be seasons when we have to toggle back and forth between strategic and practical time management. Most of us are going to need to practice an adaptability that enables us to exercise wisdom for what could never have been anticipated or, at least, was not obvious in an earlier stage of life.

Prioritize your essentials; eliminate non-essentials where possible

The first issue is not as much how we are managing our time and structuring our life as it is what we have identified as essential and important. From the outset of this book, Rusty and I have been urging all of us to thoughtfully and intentionally consider what Jesus taught us was most important and how he modeled living life in its fullest. The Bible is clear that serious people think a lot about their life and the span of their days. In the apostle Paul's letter to the Ephesians, he shared how—in light of evil's reality and the precarious nature of life—we are to *"Look carefully then how you walk, not as unwise but as wise, making the best use of the time."*[4]

Most of us want to be better at living out our values and priorities. We want a growing and more fulfilled life. We want to live more of what Jesus taught was the meaningful life. To do so, we will inevitably be moved to use our time more intentionally and be drawn—as if by the pull of gravity—toward real, honest, humble evaluation of everything we do on a regular basis. What fits with our priorities and what doesn't? What routines need to be embraced to keep us on track? Which should be eliminated?

Recognize the significance of every day

Much of life is lived without fanfare. Some might even call it boring. While there are high points and important moments, most of us have job or home responsibilities that require a certain consistency that is anything but confetti and laser light shows. Most of life is lived out, not in the race, but in the training for it. There's an old saying that "Success is where preparation meets opportunity"—while the

> Most of life is lived out, not in the race, but in the training for it.

opportunities are the exciting parts, they are difficult to anticipate, thus it is the preparation that makes the difference. As Paul wrote:

Do you not know that in a race all the runners run, but only one receives the prize? So run that you may obtain it. Every athlete exercises self-control in all things. They do it to receive a perishable wreath, but we an imperishable. So I do not run aimlessly; I do not box as one beating the air. But I discipline my body and keep it under control, lest after preaching to others I myself should be disqualified.[5]

We can all benefit from reflecting and assessing how we are living our lives and spending our days. It's not just what is on our calendars, as Rusty mentioned in the last chapter, but what is there *every week*. We tend to overestimate what we can accomplish in a day, but underestimate what we can accomplish in a year.

Is a lot of our day or week, for example, being frittered away on things that are either nonessential—or worse— unhealthy? Damaging to our soul and well-being? Every now and then, we should reset our approach to how we are organizing our activities.

If we believe certain things are crucial to a meaningful life, then it's imperative that we reflect those priorities in the way we use our time in our daily and weekly living. If we don't have congruency between what we value and how we spend our hours, then we will most likely start to feel discouraged and frustrated because of the disconnect.

The good news is that no matter where we are, we can reorganize and begin again.

AN APP FOR THIS: DEVELOPING MEANINGFUL ROUTINES

Thanks, Terry, for digging into Jesus's rhythms a bit and showing us how he put first things first, living wholeheartedly into the reason his Father sent him to the earth. Would that we could walk half as gracefully as Jesus did in the things God has called us to do and be.

Why only half? Because it's not easy. It's one thing to say that we love God with all of our heart, soul, mind, and strength and that we love others as ourselves, but it's a giant step further to put those loves into practice. Of course, Jesus did it brilliantly, probably also from his youth (Joseph and Mary surely had to tell others that they had the "perfect" child and teenager). He put loving his Father into his daily and weekly rhythms and then built everything around what he valued the most. He truly suffered at various points in his life, but the meaning he was living for made that suffering secondary.

It wasn't that he ignored his earthly responsibilities. Jesus did all that was required of him by heaven and earth, but he did it with obedience to and in fellowship with his heavenly Father. He also did it with eternity ever in mind, knowing everything had its place and significance in the grand scheme of his mission.

Getting what we want out of our own individual lives among all of our obligations demands similar dedication—loves first, always, and then all our other responsibilities and aspirations. There are habits and routines that, if we master the skills and knowledge of them, will help us accomplish great things down the road, even if we're not sure what those great things might be quite yet. Managing our mornings, developing workout habits to keep ourselves in shape, mastering how

> There are habits and routines that, if we master the skills and knowledge of them, will help us accomplish great things down the road, even if we're not sure what those great things might be quite yet.

we handle our money, how we treat and encourage other people, and especially how we love God will all help us be more in control of the life we want to live and better able to handle things when the universe seems to want to "stress test" our commitments, capabilities, priorities, and values.

You may have heard it said that if we want to make sure we do something, then we should do it first thing in the morning. If there are time-wasting rabbit holes we don't want to get sucked down, then we should make sure that they don't happen until an allotted place sometime when we're more open to distraction, like during a break or commuting somewhere on a bus or train. Of course, as you are reading this, you might have just finished a time management book that told you just the opposite. Maybe there is no perfect answer?

As for me, I've spent a good deal of time thinking about how I "boot up" my day and I've found it quite valuable. I am confident that we all expect our phones, tablets, and computers to bootup the same way each time when we turn them on. Can you imagine the havoc that it would cause if, one day, when your phone boots up, Facebook opens, then the next day, Spotify takes over and starts playing music, and then the next day, something else grabs your phone's attention first? Then once we've cleared whatever unexpectedly popped up first, we can't find our email icon or that file we've been working on, because they've been moved to a new place? Then imagine the next day when your home screen starts rotating pictures from your photo app? I know what I'd want to do—I'd want to throw the phone out the window and go find one that does the same thing, every time, every day, without deviation.

As I'm writing this, I can look to the wall in front of my desk where I can see my daily "bootup" routine. (Yes, I wrote it down and keep it in front of me so I wouldn't forget it.) It includes all the things I think are important before I get to anything else. (And let me confess up front—I almost never get through the entire routine and almost never actually get it in the same order, though I really, really try.) My ideal morning would go something like this:

1. Walk Theo (our French Bulldog) and feed him.

2. Hydrate (I intermittent fast so no food before noon).

3. Spend time in the Bible (intentional reading) and in prayer.

4. Listen to/watch an audio/video devotional/meditation (Abide, Rise and Shine, Headspace, etc.) and spend some time contemplating it.

5. Read the news.

6. Write my purposed worKING blog.[6]

7. Workout (depending on the day—run, gym, or swim).

8. Off to email, Zoom, or whatever work and engagements I have scheduled for that day.

When it comes to booting up your day, one size fits one and how you boot up will look quite different from how I do. However, I do think that we can share a few categories of routines that might make it easier for all of us to find that personal rhythm of grace, which is what we are looking for after all.

What if we looked at all the things in our lives that we want to love, and created a plan for loving them properly? Then, once you have identified those things, you can create a routine and plug it into your calendar and reminders—like remembering a sibling's birthday or your anniversary or your annual review at work—and you can make sure you get to them on a regular basis. I like to put things into my calendar on a daily, weekly, monthly, quarterly, and annual basis.

Creating such routines, rituals, and rhythms is the only way we can be sure we touch on what is most important to us on a regular basis. It is part and parcel of building an operating system for life, a part of a platform that we can fall back upon in the times when other things crowd in trying to take their place (which *always* happens). Only by keeping our disciplines at the core of our bootup process—at least somewhere in our week where they cannot be displaced with something else—are we going to be able to systematically keep our loves in order.

I use a system that looks something like this:

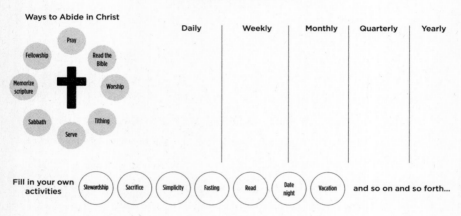

Making the Most of an Intentional Spiritual Routine
Establish Your Rituals

Now, I don't want to be overly prescriptive, but there are certain activities we associate with spiritual duty and godly discipline as Terry mentioned above—or to use the terms we've been using, with ways of loving God. Then, you also have other loves, like your spouse, exercise, reading, playing something (golf, basketball, tennis, or video games), going on a vacation, volunteering, mentoring (or being mentored), or other "loves" you feel are important, but don't necessarily fit into your daily or weekly routine. Once you have a list of all of those activities, you could drop them into your dailies, weeklies, monthlies, quarterlies, and yearlies to look something like this:

Your Intentional Spiritual Routine could look something like this:

Establish Your Rituals

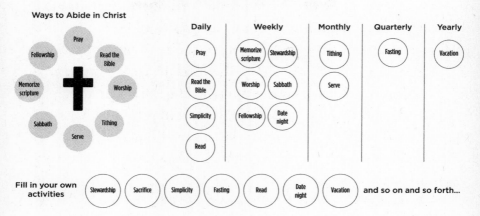

Then this could be a plan you review and adjust on a regular basis (say, monthly), filling in specifics and dropping in dates when you will do each. This is just one way of doing it, but without a plan, we'll be less likely to stick to our loves when push comes to shove. Having our priorities in writing allows firm ground from which we can exert leverage on who we are becoming as we grow.

On the other hand, it's always worth giving some thought to what we're going to exclude from our schedule. For example, I grew up a TV kid (and still am at heart). I *love* TV and could watch anything. I was always fascinated with whatever was on the screen. Even today, when I am exhausted and I want go into rest mode, I will sit down in front of the TV and watch whatever piques my interest first; a dangerous thing with Netflix, Hulu, and every other streaming service out there now allowing us to stream and binge whatever catches our fancy. It's easy to check out while such shows take us places we never would have chosen to go.

And it's not just TV. It can happen while listening to music, playing games, reading a book, surfing the internet for the next funny animal video, playing a sport, or whatever helps us relax and refuel. Whatever the form of entertainment, it is important that we ensure that the "fuel" for our minds is furthering our ability to stay mentally strong and expanding, not constricting us, or ever eating away at our souls.

Remember the computer programming adage: "Garbage in is garbage out."

Today, as I look back, I realize it is more the books I have read that I am most grateful for than the shows I have watched every episode of. They are what has made me a better leader, a better husband, a better friend, and exposed me to more different worldviews than anything else I've done. (We hope this book is doing the same for you!) While I could probably match you question for question in a trivia contest about seventies and eighties TV programs, so what? I would have been so much better off if I defaulted to reading first and TV second instead of the other way around. It's something I often remind myself before I reach for the remote. (If you have the same issue, consider the 20-Second Rule from *The Happiness Advantage*. Put a book where you usually place your remote and your remote at least a twenty-second walk away. Little adjustments can make big differences!)

That said, it's okay to be entertained. Not everything has to be a documentary or a self-improvement video. We all need down time. Just be aware of what you're doing and what you expect to get out of it by the time you unplug and go to bed. Are you better for it? Or at least somewhat refreshed? Or does what you've just watched or "doom scrolled" leave you with your skin crawling and feeling worse about yourself? Remember, this is your *re*-creation time—what are you creating or rejuvenating with it? Being thoughtful in this area demands being ready sometimes to saying "no" to the show that everyone else thinks we should watch. Plus, there are several things not worth absorbing into our spirits, no matter how popular or enticing they are.

There's another old adage, "When is the best time to plant a tree? Twenty years ago. When is the second-best time? Today." Forming a rhythm with desirable habits and routines earlier rather than later is something you'll never regret. And it's never too late to start.

> Forming a rhythm with desirable habits and routines earlier rather than later is something you'll never regret.

REFLECTION QUESTIONS

1. Take a quick inventory of your weekly activities (if needed, create a spreadsheet with the 168 hours of the week listed to track how you spend your time over the next two weeks). Is there a regular place for all of your "loves" in your weekly schedule?

2. Read Genesis 1–2. What is the life you see God creating for humanity through his work? How do you see God's work here and what he assigned to Adam and Eve relating to your work?

3. How do you manage your schedule? What tools or habits have worked the best for you that you might recommend to others?

4. Look back to Rusty's ideal morning list on pages 92–93. What values do you see exemplified in his list? What would your ideal morning look like?

5. How do you manage your mornings? How do you celebrate the Sabbath? What are the most important activities that should show up in your schedule every week?

SIX

AN INTENTIONAL LIFE

> "For which of you, desiring to build a tower, does not first sit down and count the cost, whether he has enough to complete it? Otherwise, when he has laid a foundation and is not able to finish, all who see it begin to mock him, saying, 'This man began to build and was not able to finish.'"
>
> —*Luke 14:28–30*

Jesus never minced words about the cost of following him. He likened it to *"taking up your cross daily"*[1] and *"laying down your life."*[2] While I (Terry) believe Jesus knew his disciples would to be willing to die for him (all but John were martyred), I think he was really more concerned with how they would live. It's one thing to say, "I want to give my life to Jesus," but in a practical, day-to-day sense, what's that look like? What does it mean for how we spend the hours of our day, earn our living, contribute to society, and interact with our families and neighbors?

Jesus made it clear where he placed the accent of life when he asked, *"For what does it profit a man if he gains the whole world and loses or forfeits himself?"*[3] This question forces us to evaluate our priorities and think of our life construction in the light of his love and truth—just what are we building with our lives? Who are we becoming? What do we hope to leave behind?

God planted a sense of purpose and destiny in each of our hearts when we were conceived, and those are reflected in our talents and yearnings. We realize this calling a little like Eric Liddell recognized God had called him to be an Olympian in the classic film, *Chariots of Fire*. In a scene where Liddell explains to his sister that he will only accept his call to be a missionary to China after running in the 1924 Olympics for England, he says: "I believe that God made me for a purpose: for China. But he also made me *fast*. And when I run, I feel his pleasure. To give it up would be to hold him in contempt. You were right. It's not just fun. To win is to honor him." I believe God calls us to walk with a similar attitude daily while always knowing there is an eternity to win.

Just as it was for Liddell, accomplishing this calling is no foregone conclusion. There's nothing automatic about feeling "called" to win an Olympic medal (Liddell won a gold in the 400m* and a bronze in the 200m). It requires discipline and demands preparation.

---

* Interestingly, Liddell only ran in the 400m because he withdrew from the 100m, which is where he'd qualified. He did so because the heats for the 100m were on a Sunday, and he held Sundays sacred as a Sabbath. Of course, that, as they say, is another story.

One of the first applications of our faith code we probably need—now that we've established what our foundation will be—is a sort of life GPS that will help us plot our course toward the destination God has for us, even if we're not completely sure of where we're ultimately heading. Very few are given a clear roadmap to their destiny. But we do need a compass of sorts—something we can check to verify we are still headed in the right direction. We should also formulate some itinerary of the overall journey, even if we're only concerned with today's next step.

Just what does a well-lived, loving life look like anyway?

YOU ARE HERE—WHY?

In Luke 14, Jesus outlines what it means to follow him:

> *"For which of you, desiring to build a tower, does not first sit down and count the cost, whether he has enough to complete it? Otherwise, when he has laid a foundation and is not able to finish, all who see it begin to mock him, saying, 'This man began to build and was not able to finish.'"*[4]

This is a tough passage for anyone unsure about building their life on the platform of the Great Commandment, but to put God first is the foundation that allows us to build what Paul called, *"that which is truly life."*[5] It is to rely, in all situations, upon God's grace, a grace German pastor and anti-Nazi activist Dietrich Bonhoeffer described as *costly*: "It is costly because it costs a man his life, and it is grace because it gives a man the only true life."[6]

The hope is—and I believe it comes out of a call from our hearts as well—that we build lives of love, joy, abundance, and significance. That, day by day, we would do things that matter and make a difference—that we might go into our days boldly, filled with a sense that what we set our hands to is important in at least some small way, and that we and some around us will be all the better at the end of the day for us having stayed the course. As we grow through the seasons of life and improve at seeing God's clues about our general direction, we should also get better at doing meaningful things.

Solomon wrote: *"For everything there is a season, and a time for every matter under heaven."*[7] I like to think of life in terms of natural seasons. I think there is value in considering the full length of our lives as having a spring, a summer, an autumn, and a winter, and thinking in terms of each season being twenty to twenty-five years.

> I think there is value in considering the full length of our lives.

Taking this a step further, I think each season of life also has micro-seasons: an early, a middle, and a late. Like the seasons of the year—with each year being slightly different just as each life is—one changes into the other almost imperceptibly. Days in late summer can feel no different from those of early fall. When you're in late spring, it can feel just like summer. But there does come a day when you know you have transitioned from one to the other. There is a time when the days start feeling longer again after winter solstice. There is a day when putting on a sweater is necessary or wearing shorts is or isn't really an option.

Each season also has its own distinct characteristics. If we think of starting in springtime, early spring—childhood— is distinct from pre-adolescence and early adolescence (mid-spring) as well as late spring or early adulthood (our early twenties). Summer is usually marked by decisions about family, career, buying or renting a home, and the like. Fall is filled with reevaluating purpose, how to give to those in the spring and summer of their lives, harvesting from the career "seeds" planted in spring and summer, and making provisions for winter. Winter is about golden years of mentorship and harvest—giving back and hopefully enjoying the long-term effects of investment, learning, and contribution.

Moses wrote one psalm, which is Psalm 90. In it, he writes, *"Teach us to number our days / that we may get a heart of wisdom."*[8] From time to time I think it is helpful to *"number our days"* and ask what season we are in in terms of our overall lives. What is different for us now from the last season? What should we be doing to prepare for the next? What has this journey been like for others, and what can we learn from them? Given our present season, what are reasonable and realistic expectations for what we want to accomplish, and what wisdom have we garnered that we could share?

Jesus often spoke about reflecting on our lives, our values, and God's perspective on living well and fully. This reflection is a big part of determining the best way to spend our days. Like an architect and builder considering the construction of a tower, how do we build a vibrant flourishing life, and what phase should we be in, given our season, in that construction? Sometimes there is a need to take everything back down to its foundation and start anew, wiser for whatever has happened before. Other times there is a need to seek advice of those who have already built well so that our construction can better stand and be a blessing to others. Are we in an early, middle, or latter phase? Or are we in a transition?

Transition from one season to the next is often where things can go off the rails for us. Transition is difficult because we long for the comfort of what we've been used to in the past and are fearful of whether we'll be able to handle the expectations of the future. Times when we start work, get a promotion, get married, have children, transition our children from one stage of their lives to another, start

> Transition from one season to the next is often where things can go off the rails for us.

new projects, and so on, all create conversion periods where the future will be different from the past to some degree, and the stakes for success or failure are higher. It's important to recognize and mark such times and be aware both that we need to rise toward potential, but also that there will be transitions beyond them that will demand even more of us—and also be filled with even greater potential rewards.

Once we identify our season, we must be intentional about how we live in it. Different seasons have different priorities. Our callings in one season could look quite different from the last, even though many things remain the same. Becoming a parent is different from living as newlyweds. Changing jobs could bring a completely different understanding of your calling or fulfill a completely different aspect from what you lived in the last season. Injuries or age completely reset the lives of professional athletes. A change in season may demand heading for a completely different port of call rather than simply recalibrating the course toward a destination you've had in mind since your youth. There may also be a greater overarching destiny that ties what looks like completely different purposes into one.

Because life is challenging, when seasons change it's easy to resist that change and default into the negative rather than choose new positives. It's very easy to become dissatisfied and fixated on what others have rather than being grateful and looking for the blessing in new unique circumstances. If we do anything less, it often undermines our ability to embrace what the Lord has for us. We don't want to live in denial. We want to live honestly and be able to embrace the complexity, intricacies, and joys of life. It's easy to look to the past or the future as the places where life was or will be better and miss the significance of the place and season where God is working with, in, and hopefully, through us.

I like how Paul wrote about this process to the Corinthians:

So we do not lose heart. Though our outer self is wasting away, our inner self is being renewed day by day. For this light momentary affliction is preparing for us an eternal weight of glory beyond all comparison, as we look not to the things that are seen but to the things that are unseen. For the things that are seen are transient, but the things that are unseen are eternal.[9]

"So we do not lose heart." What a great way to start. Life has a way of getting us to lose heart, of thinking our best days are

behind us, of feeling beaten down so that it's hard to move forward. Often, we have very legitimate reasons for feeling that way—the hand life deals us can often be lacking, but it's still up to us to play it well. There are going to be things in life that can be crushing and disappointing. I've talked with people in their summer and autumn years who are still struggling with things they experienced or choices they made in the springtime of their lives. Many are things others did and they had no power over.

But there is healing available—we are *"renewed day by day"* if we allow God to work in our lives. There are greater things ahead if we choose to build our lives on faith, hope, and love today—the things that are unseen—rather than let the transient things of this world weigh us down and hijack our destinies.

Jesus's question—"What shall it profit a person if they gain the world but lose their soul?"—forces us to evaluate our priorities and think of life construction in the light of eternity. If we are going to do that, here are some good things to keep in mind.

Jesus thought like an architect and lived like an artist.

Each season of our lives provides ample and unique opportunities for joy and accomplishment. Seasonal life growth, like most growth, shows up in the myriad of choices we make on a daily, weekly, monthly, and annual basis. The priorities of our life are revealed, or at least confirmed, by how we choose to spend our time. Big hopes and aspirations only turn into reality when we work toward them each day. As Benjamin Franklin wrote, "Dost thou love life? Then do not squander time, for that is the stuff life is made of."

Also remember the big picture. Proverbs 19:21 tells us: *"Many are the plans in the mind of a man, but it is the purpose of the Lord that will stand."* As architects we make plans, but things change. God redirects—for it is his purposes that ultimately matter more than what we think we want. As artists, we need to be able to pivot when God throws a wrench in our plans and embrace the change he is bringing to us. Ultimately, it is about being on God's trajectory, not having God bless our plans.

Jesus never let the urgent suffocate the important.

Those who don't look ahead or think beyond the immediate can fall into the trap of having their life sucked into things that demand attention over making room for quality time with loved ones or spent in daily reflection and edification. When we create systems and rhythms in our lives, we prioritize what we want to grow toward and what we value over what the world haphazardly throws at us. We won't always be able to avoid emergencies, but we can keep them from being the norm rather than the exception with some forethought, preparation, and organization.

Jesus took time to appreciate each season's beauty.

We need to take time to appreciate the unique blessing each season and stage has to offer. Part of enjoying the journey is pausing to reflect on each season's gifts. Too often we are living with our heads down and our feet moving. Every now and then, at least once a week, we would do well to

> Too often we are living with our heads down and our feet moving.

enjoy the gifts we have been given. Remember every season has its own blessings—that's why we call it "the present." (Okay, I know, but I couldn't resist.)

No matter where you are in life, look back with gratitude and forward with anticipation. Love forgives the past, embraces the present, and hopes in the future. We have contributions to make at every age and in every season, and there is always another adventure to embark on if we are open to Christ's call.

> We have contributions to make at every age and in every season, and there is always another adventure to embark on if we are open to Christ's call.

AN APP FOR THIS: DEVELOPING AND PROTECTING OUR IP

As Terry would tell you, I've spent most of my career working in and around technology and entertainment. *The* most important and foundational part of such businesses is the development and protection of its intellectual property, often referred to as its "IP." Intellectual property can be a story, a song, a piece of art, a book, poem, article, or play, a speech, a recording, an image, a piece of hardware, a recipe or formula, an NFT, and now in college sports one's name, image, and likeness, or yes, even the lines of software code to create a program or app. Whatever is yours and you create with your mind that is unique and valuable is your intellectual property.

Terry just described how we need to be intentional with our lives of love, so I will offer up that we also need to develop another kind of IP to be successful, which I want to call an **Intentionality Plan**. Just like intellectual property, it's something that we need to create and then protect as if it were the very life blood of who we are. This personal plan becomes how we operationalize our faith code and determines how we see ourselves, as well as who we are to others.

In his classic book, *Ordering Your Private World*, pastor and author Gordon MacDonald describes the difference for those who have an Intentionality Plan and those who don't.

> Those who brought their lives into discipline or (and this is a favorite word of mine) *intentionality* would, more than likely, go on to long-term lives of fruitfulness, and their best years would be in the last half of their lives when discipline and depth paid off. And those like me, who relied heavily upon our natural giftedness, would reach some high point early in our lives and, more than likely, trail off into *averageness* for the last half of our days on earth. Of the former, it would be said, "He [or she] is a person of rich spiritual qualities." Of me, given where I was, it would be more likely be said, "Well, he certainly was a flash in the pan."[10]

So, just how do we become *intentional*?

As we'll see if we revisit our growth chart from chapter four, our Intentionality Plans emerge in four different areas of our lives: in how we recreate, in our relationships, in our vocations, and in our health.

Our recreational plan

A large part of what forms us the most is what is fun, pleasure-giving, strength-building, and enjoyable for us. We should constantly remember that, whether it is in the middle of a tough physical workout, prayer, when we hook a golf ball into the trees, walking in a park, or are engrossed in a book, we are in the process of becoming. How are we letting those moments create who we *truly* are?

Recreation is a reflection of our hearts and where we are placing our intentions. This means we need to bring intentionality into answering the heart questions of "What do you love?" and "How do you love it?" Everything we do on the outside should be a reflection of who we are in our deeper-most selves, in the parts of us that connect with God, in our spirts.

> Everything we do on the outside should be a reflection of who we are in our deeper-most selves.

Our relational plan

It might seem like a disconnect to say that our relationships are an external expression of the state of our soul, but not if you give it some thought. How often does the way we treat others have more to do with who we are on the inside than who we are relating to? I would say more often than not.

It might be best to think of those we are in relationship with in a series of concentric circles, like on a dartboard: the bullseye being our most intimate relationships (usually our immediate family and closest friends); then our extended family and those we are the most "like-minded" with; then our acquaintances: those whose names we remember, but never discuss anything deeper with than the last sporting event or what our weekend plans are. Outside of that are the people we really don't even know—for the most part you might think of them as "friends" or followers on social media, the cashier at the grocery store, and the like—people you are much more transactional with than relational.

Now that we have this "dartboard" laid out in front of us with little flags with names on them mentally placed in each ring, we have to ask ourselves the hard question: "Where are we spending our best time and giving the most of our souls?"

This may change a bit from season to season, but overall, the more central someone is to our lives, the more we should be intentional about spending time with them and investing of ourselves. If we can be known and loved by those who mean the most to us, then we are building our lives on a bedrock of deep significance.

Our vocational plan

I use the term "vocation" here rather than "job" or "career" with reason. To live a fulfilling and flourishing life, our work needs to be much more than just a way to make money to pay our bills, finance our fun, and fund the causes we care about. There should be a sense of calling to what we do for a living. (A root of *vocation* is an ancient word for "voice" implying that someone called us to it, as well as that it is an expression of who we really are.) We work for many reasons, but in reality, we should be working for one core reason: To express what earlier Christians called the *imago dei*—that we would be the "image of God" to the world around us. How did Dr. Martin Luther King Jr. describe it?

> All labor that uplifts humanity has dignity and importance and should be undertaken with painstaking excellence. If a man is called to be a street sweeper, he should sweep streets even as a Michelangelo painted, or Beethoven composed music, or Shakespeare wrote poetry. He should sweep streets so well that all the hosts of heaven and earth will pause to say, "Here lived a great street sweeper who did his job well."[11]

We are to work with purpose and our purpose should be expressed through the work that we do. So should utilizing and maximizing our gifts, skills, and talents, turning all of that into a plan so that we can find the best expression of who God created each of us to be.

Our health plan

Perhaps it's easiest to see the importance of having an IP for health when we think of our physical bodies. A story told to me of a CEO and co-founder of a company is a perfect example of this. One day his co-founder sat him down and told him that he wanted to give him some feedback. He then proceeded to lay into him about being a "terrible CEO and a horrible example of leadership."

His co-founder told him, "You've gained forty pounds, you drink caffeine from morning to night, you don't eat right, and you smoke cigarettes like they are going out of style (which they have, by the way). You work sixteen hours a day, seven days a week, and you don't sleep more than four or five hours a night."

The CEO was about to do the Silicon Valley Tech-Bro thing and say, "So what's wrong with that?" in his defense, when his co-founder said, "Just look around. *Everyone* else here is doing the same because they look up to you and you are their example. Is that what you want for our employees?"

That last statement hit the CEO between the eyes. He changed his intentions! First, he put a scheduled calendar hour in his day, every day, to exercise. He quit smoking and he started eating better. He also added "Be in the best shape to lead at my best" to his job description.

We cast a shadow as leaders that others will walk in. So even if getting into shape so that you can one day walk down the aisle with your granddaughter at her wedding seems too far off for you or you really don't care about hiking the Camino de Santiago at age seventy, look at the example you want to be to

> We cast a shadow as leaders that others will walk in.

your friends and colleagues around you. It might be time to get yourself in shape for someone else, even if not just for yourself. (And, again, that applies in all the areas of our lives: spirit, soul, vocation, financial, relational, etc.)

Our Intentionality Plan is really important if we want to live a fulfilled life. It starts with our intentions in the areas of life that we love; then, if we wrap a plan around those intentions, we might be pleasantly surprised by how our lives get better and better.

But it will never happen if we're not *intentional* about it.

REFLECTION QUESTIONS

1. Given where you are in your life right now, what are the challenges and objectives that you have that are different from those you've had in the past? What are you hoping for in the next season of your life and what will you need to accomplish to get there?

2. Read Luke 9:23–26 and 14:26–33. What costs do you face by taking up the cross of Christ and following his commandments? How will you stay strong in remembering the most important obligations in your life?

3. What are some aspirations you have in life? How do those relate to what you sense is God's calling for you?

4. Take a few minutes and write something about your intentions under each of the four categories of IP Rusty outlined: spiritual, physical, vocational, and relational. What can you do to keep these intentions front of mind in the days, weeks, and years to come?

5. How will you apply the love of God in each of these areas? (Remember the acronym, love CARES from chapter three.)

PART III

APPLYING THE FRAMEWORK

"Do not lay up for yourselves treasures on earth, where moth and rust destroy and where thieves break in and steal, but lay up for yourselves treasures in heaven, where neither moth nor rust destroys and where thieves do not break in and steal. For where your treasure is, there your heart will be also."

—*Matthew 6:19–21*

Practice doesn't make perfect. Practice makes permanent.

—John Cleveland

SEVEN

YOU WERE CREATED TO INNOVATE

For we are God's masterpiece. He has created us anew in Christ Jesus, so we can do the good things he planned for us long ago.

—*Ephesians 2:10* NLT

In their book, *Every Good Endeavor*, pastor and bestselling author Tim Keller (with Katherine Leary Alsdorf) point out that the Judeo-Christian creation story is unique among creation stories in many ways. In the Babylonian story, the world is created as the result of a cosmic war and is forged out of the loser's remains. According to the Greeks, the world emerged through a succession of "ages," the original paradise holding such abundance that neither man nor god needed to labor. Others follow similar themes, the world being either forged from the fire of conflict or falling from an idyllic state of leisure and ease—the ultimate four-hour workweek, so to speak.

According to the Bible, however, creation was the result of God going to work. As the authors of *Every Good Endeavor* write, "Creation . . . is not the aftermath of a battle but the plan of a craftsman. God made the world not as a warrior digs a trench but as an artist makes a masterpiece."[1] In contrast to the Greek story,

> Repeatedly the first chapters of the book of Genesis describe God at "work," using the Hebrew *mlkh*, the word for ordinary human work. . . .
>
> In the beginning then, God worked. Work was not a necessary evil that came into the picture later, or something human beings were created to do but that was beneath the great God himself. No, God worked for the sheer joy of it. Work could not have a more exalted inauguration.[2]

Once creation was set in motion (as we discussed a bit back in chapter five), God promptly turned the "family business" of taking care of creation over to Adam and Eve. They were to *"Prosper! Reproduce! Fill Earth! Take charge! Be responsible for fish in the sea and birds in the air, for every living thing that moves on the face of Earth."*[3] Then he rested, taking a day to look back over it all, admire what he had accomplished, and consider what he might do in the next week—in partnership with the trustees he had just appointed to oversee his creation to further take chaos and turn it into new, helpful products and practices.

According to the Bible, we are all made in the image of God. We bear the divine imprint. The scriptures make it clear that even in our (sin-impacted) brokenness, we human beings still reflect our Creator. There are "God seeds" in all of us—desires for him, yes, but also desires for meaningful work, for purpose, the desire to make things more orderly and useful, and to help society be a just and fair place for all. We "work out" the gift of redemption we experienced when we declared Jesus our Lord and Savior. We hunger for and find fulfillment in "good work." We see the potential God imbued into our world and each other at creation and we want to bring that potential forth, just as Adam and Eve did before the Fall.

What does it then mean that we are to reflect his image to the world? How do our entrepreneurial and creative endeavors bear his image? How are we to bless society and the earth through what we are uniquely gifted and empowered to do?

JESUS, THE GET-THINGS-DONE ENTREPRENEUR

There was an incident at the very beginning of Jesus's ministry when his mother came to him with a somewhat audacious request. I (Terry) have always found it fascinating. Evidently, the host of a wedding they were attending in Cana had run out of wine for the guests. In that time, it would have been considered an especially embarrassing development. It was a blunder that could give a family a reputation for being cheap or negligent for years to come!

So Mary, who was evidently very close to the family, asked Jesus to intervene—well, she kind of asked. According to the scriptures, she simply came to him and presented him with the problem: "They have no wine."[4] Mary knew her son to be a problem solver—in her mind, all that was needed was for him to be presented with the problem, and he would provide a solution.

Knowing Jesus as we do, that makes perfect sense, but Mary didn't know him at that moment the way we do today. According to the scriptures, what followed was the first miracle Jesus ever performed.

> In every problem, there is an opportunity to innovate.

In every problem, after all, there is an opportunity to innovate.

"We're not going to make payroll this week" can turn into a catastrophe or a brilliant new pricing structure that encourages enough clients to pay early so no one goes without getting paid. The constant crashing of a program leads to an ingenious new bit of code that produces stability. A niche problem solved through a lateral use of technology becomes the basis for a new business. A derelict park known for drug dealing and prostitution becomes a neighborhood cleanup project that blossoms into a closer-knit, more vibrant, and vigilant community. A flaw in a delivery system becomes an entirely new process for managing the warehousing and distribution of products across several industries. A neighborhood of closed storefronts and rampant unemployment becomes a string of restaurant businesses known for sourcing local produce and hiring and developing local talent.

I could go on and on—living in the Bay Area we constantly hear stories like this coming out of Silicon Valley and other parts of the city. Such problem-solving has become a hallmark of life in the Bay Area, which has not only fed the local economy but also the national one.

And I don't believe it's too much of a stretch to see Jesus as this kind of problem-solving, entrepreneurial craftsman. I can imagine, as a local tradesman, he was constantly solving problems for people, whether it was a door that didn't quite close, constructing a dining room table for a large family, or negotiating an agreement between guilds of local merchants. I think Jesus, at thirty years old, would have been right in the heart of his local community being both a solid business-person and a contributing citizen. I could easily see him as someone with a reputation for getting things done.

It was because of this that his mother came to him with that tricky problem: They've run out of wine. Perhaps not a big deal, given time, but the wedding feast was at its height, and it wasn't like they could wait for next-day delivery. Perhaps she thought he would call his friend the wine seller to open up his shop for a DoorDash of the times. Perhaps she thought he knew a wine merchant who might open his shop just to help them out. Whatever it was she thought, it ended with Jesus solving the problem in a miraculous way.

Jesus knew the difficulty of the task, however, more reasonably than she did. He knew she was asking for a miracle. *"Woman, what does this have to do with me? My hour has not yet come."*[5]

Mary's response? *"His mother said to the servants, 'Do whatever he tells you.'"*[6] She knew he'd come up with something— though I imagine she was just as surprised at what happened next as those servants were when they dipped into the water jugs and took wine to the master of the feast!

As Rusty pointed out earlier, one of the attributes of the God kind of love is that it is creative. When God's love is presented with a problem, it innovates a solution. I believe this is at least part of what Jesus meant when he said:

> When God's love is presented with a problem, it innovates a solution.

"Have faith in God. Truly, I say to you, whoever says to this mountain, 'Be taken up and thrown into the sea,' and does not doubt in his heart, but believes that what he says will come to pass, it will be done for him. Therefore I tell you, whatever you ask in prayer, believe that you have received it, and it will be yours."[7]

I believe that we are God's hands and feet on the earth, and more often than not, God tends to answer prayers in a way that calls the body of Christ into action. I believe medicine is a way God uses to heal and answer prayers. Oftentimes he answers prayers for finances with new jobs or ideas for a "witty invention"[8] that could be developed into a business.

When we see problems on the earth and wonder why God hasn't done something about them, I think we are missing the point. God doesn't respond to need; he responds to faith. We are the ones who are supposed to bring those needs to him *in* faith, so that he can partner with us in innovating a solution for them. He gave the care and cultivating of the earth over to us; if there are problems, he expects us to answer them, though he is also more than willing to partner with us in the process if we ask. Sometimes I think that's really what he was after in the first place.

To return to the discussion in Timothy Keller and Katherine Leary Alsdorf's book, *Every Good Endeavor*, not only was work a part of God's original plan in the garden, but it is also part of God's new plan through the gospel. We fall into an error that plagued the early church when we think that the salvation Jesus won through the cross was only spiritual, when we think of some work as being sacred and other work as being secular. Our work—like our money—is a tool that either promotes good and feeds abundance or extracts profit and takes advantage of the earth or others. Just as being a pastor doesn't protect a person from moral failure, running a large business doesn't condemn a person to a life of loving money and abusing workers and the environment. It's all about how we carry out our life's work.

Paul prayed that we would all *"walk in a manner worthy of the Lord, fully pleasing to him: bearing fruit in every good work and increasing in the knowledge of God."*[9] God does not call most of us to be secluded in monasteries, but to partner with him to see the good news of salvation (both spiritual and material) spread throughout the entire earth. It is the "good work" he has given us to do out of the abundance that comes from loving him.

It has often been said that we are "to be in the world," but "not of the world," a paraphrasing of part of Jesus's prayer in John 17. But what does this mean, exactly? While some values in the world are obviously in conflict with the values of God, some are more insidious, tripping us up without us even realizing it. Here are a couple of mindsets Rusty and I run into frequently that we have seen take people off course:

Spiritual things are better than material things.

Every day of creation, God proclaimed the physical things he made as "good." That hasn't changed. Things only become "bad" when we let them break the first two commandments[10] and we put our relationship with them before our relationship with God. God gave us everything in the world to enjoy, but not to make gods of. Like money, they should serve what we are doing in our lives for God, we should not serve them. We are all called to ministry on this earth—it's just that some of us serve in churches or homes while others of us serve in the marketplace. One is not better than the other—as long as we are truly doing what God has called us to do.

> We are all called to ministry on this earth—it's just that some of us serve in churches or homes while others of us serve in the marketplace.

Some kinds of work are "holier" than others.

It's long been a problem in the church that we fall into a sacred/secular split between occupations. You either go into the ministry and serve God, or you go out into the secular world to earn money or resources and sanctify it by giving it to support ministry.

It's also easy to get absorbed in thinking that white-collar (executive) work is better than blue-collar (hands-on) work, or that those who choose to work at home and care for a family are less than those who choose to work in an office, or that those who get paid more are better people than those who get paid less. While different people with different education levels or skills and talents will have different economic value to companies, they do not have different human worth, nor is there more dignity in one form of work than another (unless, of course, it is criminal or exploitive or something like that).

Every day, no matter the kind of work we do or the titles on our resume, we are responsible to God to walk in a manner pleasing to him. Our identities should be not only anchored in being his daughters and sons but also in fulfilling our individual assignments to establish our special corner of his kingdom. That means both doing "good work" and doing it in a way that reflects how Jesus loved. It also means that no matter what we are doing or creating, at the end of each day, we should be able to look back and see "that it was good" just as God did each day of his creation.

AN APP FOR THIS:
WHY NOT BE WILDLY CREATIVE?

Who co-opted the term *creative*?

One of the largest talent agencies in the world tried to own the term—Creative Artists Agency—although I (Rusty) always thought "creative artists" seemed a little redundant. It's too bad that those in the entertainment industry want us to believe that they are the "creatives" and the rest of us aren't (but then again commercials are always telling us actors aren't real people, so maybe it's fair), but nothing could be further from the truth. If God is *the* Creator and the "Innovator on High," and we are made in his image, then by default, we are creators too, even daily innovators. Have you found a better way to get work done? Explored a route that others haven't discovered yet? Utilized a kitchen gadget for something other than what it was designed for and it works like a charm? Created an efficient shortcut that makes others more productive? Drawn? Painted? Written? Composed? You get the point. We are all creators. So, *why don't we act like it?*

Again, the answer lies in what we love.

I once had the chance to meet the artist, Frank Stella, after a talk he gave at the San Francisco Museum of Modern Art. That evening, he was asked why he does what he does. He answered, "Those of us who have the burden to emulate the masters, do what I do." I have never forgotten this. He didn't say, "choice," "desire," "wish," "opportunity," or "willingness," he said, "burden." In what he said that night, I heard his *burden* was for what he loved.

Having a burden to create and innovate is how artists, entrepreneurs (whether they are designing a new smartphone or finding a new way to market pies), and the like carry themselves. It's why we have the term, "starving artist" (and many businesspeople have similar tough start stories from their early days). They are willing to starve in order to have more time to create. That might knock a bunch of us out from wanting to be called a "creative" or "innovator," but it shouldn't. I tend to think of it this way: God has given us all gifts, and while some are more pronounced in certain people than others, we all still have them. We've all been created in the image of the Ultimate Creator. Some of him is down inside each of us. It's what we love wanting to be realized. It's just a question of when and where we allow our creativity to emerge.

In the technology world, entrepreneurs start their funding pitches with "What is the problem our company is going to solve?" Regardless, whether it is a common, uncommon, big, or small problem, I love when I hear their statements, because they are rooted in an individual who is experiencing or has experienced a problem in their own lives and they just "have to" (think "burden") fix it. When we hear their "elevator pitches," the catalyst for their work is profoundly evident. They can tell their "origin stories" that start with a passion and love that developed at an early age. It is quite remarkable. And it's not only for-profit ventures that do this. Nonprofit leaders are just as passionate and will go above and beyond and give of themselves, their time, and their treasures to solve the big problems they are "burdened with" to make the world just that little bit better for the rest of us.

I'd like to propose that in order to have the kind of lives God wants us to have, that we commit to exercising our gifts of creativity and innovation by finding a problem that needs to be solved and then jumping in to bring our ideas and talents to bear. Imagine a town or city, a country, or even an entire world, where everyone took up, at a minimum, one challenge and deployed their unique creativity to solve it—then shared their solution with others. What a generosity-driven, love-oriented world that would be! How many people would have richer lives because of that one small effort? Imagine!

> Imagine a town or city, a country, or even an entire world, where everyone took up, at a minimum, one challenge and deployed their unique creativity to solve it.

So, how we do we start? We need to make room to **CREATE**.

First, find a problem that *Captures* you. What captures your heart, mind, and imagination where you know you could make a difference? What breaks your heart? It could be educational gaps, poverty, healthcare, inequalities, racial issues, safety, the elderly, the disadvantaged, or something else. (One thing we have no lack of on this fallen planet is problems!) Where could you put your skills, talents, passions, and love together to be a problem solver and innovator?

Second, decide what *Resources* you can bring with you. Resources come in many forms: time, treasures, friends, networks, talents, skills, knowledge, and so on. We've got way more things to give than just our money.

But none of these things are bottomless—they need to be stewarded—managed in a way that develops and preserves them. I remember a time at our church when we added a new campus and the Kid's Ministry asked for people to commit to serving *every* Sunday for one year. I thought it was a risky thing to ask, but the kid's pastor at the time had years of experience, so she was able to get volunteers to commit. Everyone came through, but at the end of that year, at least one person (who I still miss as she was so amazingly gifted with the kids) was so burned out and spent, that she left the church and I've never seen her since. She loved the kids, innovated, and created an amazing platform for the ministry to grow from, but she had overextended her resources of time and energy in the effort.

Budgeting up front is a great stewardship tool and makes the word "no" that much easier when the extra asks come.

These guardrails for time, money, energy, and so on, can make the difference between success and failure when it comes to solving problems around us. It's always better to go more slowly than never finish (just ask the tortoise and the hare).

Enthusiasm matters. Enthusiasm is contagious. Enthusiastic people are like magnets and fire starters in the same body. And conversely, lack of enthusiasm is so easily sniffed out and apparent that it can't be covered, or at least not for long. I have to always check myself and ask, "Where will my enthusiasm come from and how will it be renewed along the way?"

I've been fortunate to sit on a number of corporate and non-profit boards. I get asked to serve because (well, I hope because) I bring something of creativity and innovation to the table. I have also made mistakes in accepting some of these positions for the wrong reasons. I was captured by the problem to be solved and I had my resources allocated correctly, but I hadn't ensured that I was going to be able to keep my enthusiasm level high enough to at least match the enthusiasm around me. When I couldn't, I always felt like I was becoming a drain.

My litmus test now is that after a long meeting, when we all go to dinner with each other and the night drags long, will I still be enthusiastic to talk about the business or the organization when that is all they really want to talk about? When asked, will I say, "I love being on this board!"? Or will I dread those nights and being asked the question? If the latter, then I should allocate my time and resources elsewhere. And this goes for any activity or engagement I am asked to consider.

Can you be *Active* in your creativity and innovation? This seems simple, but it's really, really important. Being active means being able to do "something" that feels worthwhile. I've come to realize that when you can give someone something to do, they feel twice as engaged. We miss this too often. But, when we get it right, watch how creative, energized, and full of ideas people can become. People who hadn't sewn for years, in the midst of COVID-19, suddenly rekindled a love and became creators of some of the coolest face-protection masks. Who would have thought it? But it's what happens when we engage and are active. We know that faith without works is dead; so is passion without action. We have to be active to be fully alive and engaged in who we were created to be.

Great creativity and innovation also demand *Thoughtfulness*. Sure, any one of us can have an idea (I have journals filled with them), but to move from an idea to a reality takes a heck of a lot of thought, strategizing, and planning. I'd suggest that this thoughtfulness is an exercise to be performed with others, not a solo venture. Studies tell us that the best entrepreneurs have been those who have partners as co-founders or co-investors, not those who go it alone. Artists will often describe their muses, who turn out to be their life loves. Composers have lyricists. Writers have editors. Directors have producers. Research scientists have peer reviewers. Software engineers have testers and quality assurance. Artistic directors have managing directors. To be

> Studies tell us that the best entrepreneurs have been those who have partners as co-founders or co-investors, not those who go it alone.

thoughtful is to lean on the advice and counsel of others, sometimes a partner, but sometimes a larger cohort of people.

Drew Houston, co-founder and CEO of Dropbox, likes to say that he is the average of the five people whom he most closely surrounds himself with. Want to be better and more thoughtful as you create and innovate? Then consider, who are your five?

Finally, we have to be able to *Execute* our solution so that it will meet the need. Creativity without execution is a squandered resource. The amazing recipe that demands too many ingredients isn't going to make the menu. The backyard bench that has been created and drawn up, but doesn't fit in the spot designated, won't solve the problem of backyard barbeque seating.

I've always been fascinated with concept cars (prototypes created to show what the future might look like) that the automakers come out with each year. But how many of those cars go into production? Few, if any. What we see is their wild creativity applied to what they love, like the annual Spring fashion shows with crazy wild clothing that we never see again—not even on the red carpets. Yet, when we see something like a Tesla come to mass production, we should be more than amazed; we should be astounded. Same with an iPhone. The ability to go from idea to execution is so hard and so filled with landmines along the way that it's a wonder when anything comes to market.

Without a doubt, God would not have made us in his image if he didn't want us to be people who love to create and innovate as he does. I hope the acronym **CREATE** inspires all of us to innovate a bit on our own approach of being creative and stirs us to shake things up and find that area in our life that scratches the creativity itch.

REFLECTION QUESTIONS

1. What do you think of when you hear the word "innovation"? How much is it part of who you are and how you feel about yourself?

2. We discussed Jesus's miracle at the wedding of Cana, but where else do you see innovation show up in Jesus's life and ministry? How can we imitate his innovation? What do creativity and innovation have to do with spirituality?

3. Read Paul's prayer in Colossians 1:3–14. What are some of the things that stick out to you in this prayer? If this prayer was one you were praying for yourself or someone you know, what parts would you emphasize?

4. Let's say it's a Monday morning, and you had all the money you need to live well for the rest of your life. What would you do for the day? How does that relate to what you feel God has put you on the earth to accomplish?

5. Is there an idea, problem, or cause that captures your heart? What are areas you need to grow in so that you can have a bigger impact on this calling?

EIGHT

TRUE RICHES

As for the rich in this present age, charge them not to be haughty, nor to set their hopes on the uncertainty of riches, but on God, who richly provides us with everything to enjoy. They are to do good, to be rich in good works, to be generous and ready to share, thus storing up treasure for themselves as a good foundation for the future, so that they may take hold of that which is truly life.

—*1 Timothy 6:17–19*

Growing up as a boy in Sunday school (Terry here again), there was a Bible story that always stood out to me. We even learned a song about it, maybe you've heard it?

Zacchaeus was a wee, little man,
And a wee, little man was he.
He climbed up in a sycamore tree,
For the Lord he wanted to see.

And as the Savior came that way,
He looked up in the tree,
And he said, "Zacchaeus, you come down from there,
For I'm going to your house today.
For I'm going to your house today."

Over the years, though, Zacchaeus has become an even more interesting character to me. As we read his story in Luke 19, there are a couple of things that immediately stand out that tell us some rather darker things about this "wee little man." *"He [Jesus] entered Jericho and was passing through. And behold, there was a man named Zacchaeus. He was a chief tax collector and was rich."*[1] When we look at the history of the time, it is hard to see those two things—that he was a chief tax collector and that he was rich—as separate coincidences.

In Jesus's day tax collectors—also referred to as "publicans"—were Jewish men who collected taxes on behalf of Rome. As a result, they were some of the most despised men you would ever come across. They collected taxes from their own people for what was essentially an occupying force who taxed them at every corner of their society: income taxes, customs taxes, grain taxes, taxes and fees of every kind. Rome had a huge engine that needed to be fueled, and it was up to the conquered to supply that fuel.

Tax collectors were appointed by Rome and given authority to collect from their own people. And if, after they collected for Rome, they collected a little extra for themselves, Rome would turn a blind eye. It was a form of graft wrapped up in legality and frequently arbitrary in its application.

This created a tremendous amount of tension and deep resentment within the Jewish society of the day, which is why when the Bible refers to tax collectors like Zacchaeus, we need to realize that their culture categorized them as the most immoral of immoral people. In the eyes of the populace, they were traitors to the Jewish people—active agents working on behalf of a foreign government—and they were corrupt on top of it.

We are also told that this man, Zacchaeus, was not just a rank-and-file tax collector, but a *chief* tax collector, which means he was even more despised. He oversaw other tax collectors and probably took a cut of what they collected as well. He had a lot more power.

All that to say that Zacchaeus was not viewed as a good man, even though his name meant "pure and clean." It was the name his parents gave him, and it was ironically precisely the very opposite of what he had become occupationally. His love of power and money was outwardly evident. He was rich. He was despised. He was treated by his people as an outsider, a pariah. He had money, and the many things that money could buy, but apart from the collegiality he shared with other tax collectors, he was lonely and discontented, hungry for something better, and seemingly locked into a lifestyle that seemed certain to define his destiny.

That is, until he met Jesus.

GOD OR MONEY?

Zacchaeus had heard about Jesus, who was a bit of a celebrity at the time, and he had heard of the unconventional ways of this famous Nazarene. Zacchaeus heard Jesus would be passing through town and went to where he thought Jesus would be, just hoping to catch a glimpse of him as he passed by. As Luke tells it in his Gospel: *"And he was seeking to see who Jesus was, but on account of the crowd he could not, because he was small in stature. So he ran on ahead and climbed up into a sycamore tree to see him, for he was about to pass that way."*[2]

Here, we see a couple more things.

We learn of Zacchaeus's determination in wanting to see Jesus. He was so short and the crowd so intense that he had to get creative. He spotted a sycamore tree on the route and decided to climb it (rather ingenious if you ask me). Then we read: *"And when Jesus came to the place, he looked up and said to him, 'Zacchaeus, hurry and come down, for I must stay at your house today.' So he hurried and came down and received him joyfully."*[3]

Jesus's actions toward this man had to be a bit of a surprise—everybody was at least a little shocked and caught off guard. How could Jesus associate with such a man, let alone eat with such a cold-hearted, traitorous crook? What is Jesus doing?

I'm sure even Zacchaeus was caught off guard. "Me? Really? Are you serious? Wow! Okay. Um, just let me get out of this tree!"

And what did the disciples think? They're not mentioned, but I have to believe they were also caught off guard. "What is the Lord up to? He's doing it again, isn't he?"

The only thing the scriptures tell us for sure is: *"And when they [the crowd] saw it, they all grumbled, 'He has gone in to be the guest of a man who is a sinner.'"*[4]

It had to be a blight on Jesus's character. They were unhappy that Jesus would allow such a man to be his host, but Jesus had his reasons.

How the conversation in Zacchaeus's home went during that visit, we cannot say. The Bible does not record much of it. But the outcome we do know: Somewhere along the way Zacchaeus decided to make a change. His loves got reordered that day, *"And Zacchaeus stood and said to the Lord, 'Behold, Lord, the half of my goods I give to the poor. And if I have defrauded anyone of anything, I restore it fourfold.'"*[5]

> Somewhere along the way Zacchaeus decided to make a change. His loves got reordered that day.

Zacchaeus demonstrated that his heart has been impacted by Jesus's embrace. What action most demonstrates his internal impact? In Zacchaeus's case, it's financial restitution and a turn toward generosity. His love of money was suddenly eclipsed by a much greater love, and he was willing to give it all away for the sake of being right with God.

Jesus's reaction? He sees this and declares: *"Today salvation has come to this house, since he also is a son of Abraham. For the Son of Man came to seek and to save the lost."*[6]

Now, all these years later, looking at the same story I used to sing about as a boy, I see three very significant lessons.

1. Jesus wants our loves, regardless of our financial circumstances.

In this story, we come to understand Jesus as someone who we would enjoy spending time with and who is kind, but also relentlessly honest. He cares about whether we are interested or open to dialogue and exchange. He wants to be deeply involved in our loves. He is willing to intrude upon our ordinary to make possible the extraordinary. The Bible later expounds on this characteristic: *"Look! I stand at the door and knock. If you hear my voice and open the door, I will come in, and we will share a meal together as friends."*[7]

One of the underrated pleasures of life is eating together with friends and family. I love the fact that Jesus invites himself over to our homes for dinner—I call it *a holy intrusion.*

2. Welcoming Jesus's presence often creates turbulence that primes us for an overflow of grace, repentance, and breakthrough.

Not all internal churning is bad. Wrestling with who we are, what we love, and what we have done in the past can be beneficial. It can cause us to focus our attention on what we need to change in order to have a more flourishing life.

As we mentioned earlier, Luke doesn't record much of the nature of the conversation between Jesus and Zacchaeus. All we know is that Zacchaeus clearly was struggling to come to terms with some things, and the result was an open heart and a newly generous nature.

So it is with us when we let Jesus in.

Sometimes, we think something is wrong because we are bothered—especially as we seek to follow Jesus more closely. There have been times when reading the Bible can be the opposite of peace-inducing. It can unsettle us. It can stir a sense of discontent within us. It can prod and pry into the inner depths of our hearts. It can create a kind of conviction that causes us to consider the change or changes Jesus is inviting us to make, just as his conversation with Zacchaeus did for the "wee little man."

Jesus didn't condemn Zacchaeus for his past actions or lifestyle. Instead, he influenced Zacchaeus to change so that his loves would reflect God's presence in his life. In this way, Zacchaeus changed himself in a way that could potentially change his entire industry.

If we let him in, Jesus will do the same for us. There is a breakthrough he wants to birth us into—a new wellspring of life and joy within us that he wants to let out. We need only "get out of our tree" and let him in to experience this.

3. Spending time with Jesus will challenge our perspective of wealth and generosity.

Money isn't evil, but it's a very poor replacement for the fulfillment found in Jesus alone. Jesus even said, *"You cannot serve God and money."*[8] Serving God will impact what we do with our money, possessions, and resources. It means, what we have shouldn't have us. Financial success or failure, "In God We

> Serving God will impact what we do with our money, possessions, and resources. It means, what we have shouldn't have us.

Trust" as a way of life should always take precedence over trusting in the paper these words are printed on.

Zacchaeus decided to shift how he managed his wealth to restore anything he had gained illegitimately and then be generous with whatever he had left. In other words, a real relationship with Jesus and true repentance will show up in how we manage our income and in generosity with what we have. (Remember the wallet test Rusty shared earlier?)

Jesus in our lives will affect the way we work, conduct our business with others, and manage our resources. It will affect our generosity. It will impact our ethics, morals, and life choices. It will transform our definition and understanding of success. It will revolutionize how we work through pain, suffering, disappointment, and delayed gratification. It will bolster our kindness and generosity, and how we view and relate to people.

In short, it will change everything—but always change it for the better!

The day Zacchaeus met Jesus and welcomed him into his house, Zacchaeus learned the true value of money and what it was good for. It changed him forever.

AN APP FOR THIS:
RICH LIVING

Terry just explored wealth and gave us a thoughtful biblical approach to what it should mean to us. But, as he alluded, it's not easy. The messages that we are sent in work life and our communities is that wealth is a pursuit without an end. We might call it an endless unrequited love affair. Rockefeller was infamous for his answer to the question, "How much is enough?" His answer? "Just a little more." So goes the world. Enough is never enough.

I think, though, in the ultimatum God gives here—that you can't serve God *and* money—there is another clue. The correct choice is pretty easy: We want to love and serve God. So that leaves us with figuring out our relationship with money (because the only other option is to go hide in the mountains, grow and hunt your own food, and live off the grid—having nothing to do with money isn't really an option). Besides, having money or not having it has nothing

> Any one of us who has ever had to scramble for rent money at some time in our life knows that that's serving money just as much as thinking we need "just a little bit more" to be happy.

to do with serving it or not serving it. Any one of us who has ever had to scramble for rent money at some time in our life knows that that's serving money just as much as thinking we need "just a little bit more" to be happy.

In a talk he did for the Faith Driven Investor conference,[9] Andy Crouch took this a step further revealing the spiritual aspects of this dichotomy. In older translations of the Bible, the word used in this verse is not *money*, but *mammon*, the name of the spirit behind the love of money. Serving God means being stewards of our resources to promote human flourishing—in establishing the kingdom of God, a place of bounty and blessing for all reflecting life in heaven. Mammon, however, is an unquenchable desire for gain. It's a miserly game of accumulation that trades natural resources for revenue, and turns people into cogs in a machine or numbers in a scheme. Serving God is creative and regenerative; serving mammon is exploitive and dehumanizing.

So then, what is the only godly, healthy relationship with money? There are only two options: Either you have nothing to do with money (which is impossible this side of heaven, even with a vow of poverty—someone still has to pay the bills), or *money serves you in your service to God.*

If money serves you, it is not what defines you, but just another tool in your arsenal to use to do good. I find it helpful to think of it like a hammer. For carpenters to do their work, a hammer is an incredibly helpful tool. It might be good to have a backup hammer or two just in case, but carpenters don't determine their self-worth on how many hammers they have. They don't stockpile hundreds, thousands, or millions of hammers just to feed their egos. If a hammer isn't working to build something, it's not really of any value. Worse, if the hammer is actually doing harm in some way, then it's been corrupted. Tools should be put to work to accomplish good things at all times.

The Bible does *not* say that money is the root of all evil, although many like to misquote and weaponize the verse that way. No, that is not right. It's the *love* of money that is the evil—literally the worshipping of it, if you will—which I believe means replacing the love we are called to have for God with the love of idle, earthly wealth. Money is indeed a problem when there is either too little or too much, but with the right amount—*enough*—it is part of God's blessings for us and faith in us to do good. Money plus the love of God can be the rewards of our work and efforts, as well as a resource to finance the blessings for our families and others God puts on our hearts.

It's easy to fall into the trap that money determines worth—that it bolsters identity—because that's how the world around us operates. Something that is more expensive is worth more, thus someone who earns more is worth more. Earning more money means having more success. In this way, what something is "worth" is an easy and readily available measure—just look at the price tag or salary or profit margin—making money an easy measure to fall back on for a questionable character. But, ultimately, it's a false indicator. The true measure of success is pleasing God, not accumulating money, but that's harder to measure. It's not a transaction you can evaluate with a dollar amount—it's a relationship. It demands a different way of thinking, judging success and value, and esteeming the world around us.

Once we have avoided the trap of thinking that money defines us—that our net worth is our identity or our value is our bottom line—and we realize that it is instead one more tool for us to use to build God's kingdom on the earth, then what does that look like?

Let me ask it this way: What is your number? What is "enough" to take care of you and your household, and enough for you to live generously? What is the number for your business to be safe and take care of its employees? Just how many hammers do you need? That then is your "enough." Everything beyond that should be put to use for building God's kingdom.

> What is "enough" to take care of you and your household, and enough for you to live generously?

Let's say, for example, you came to the end of the year, and beyond your "number" (including what you have already given, and what you have put away in retirement and savings for your family and your business), you had an extra $10,000. What is the godly thing to do with that?

You could give it to your church or a charity of some kind. They could definitely benefit from that money. But what if you invested that money in a business that provided, say, twenty jobs in Africa, India, or an economically depressed part of your own country? What if you had an idea where you could take that $10,000 and turn it into $100,000 over the next five years and then give that? What if you created a fund with it that blessed your employees when they had unexpected hospital bills or other emergencies? What if you used it to hire a part-time chaplain for your business to minister to your employees?

Which of these is the right thing to do with your overflow? The easy answer is: The one God tells you to do. Of course, that means inviting God into your finances and walking with him in a way that enables a new adventure of creating something with God using money as a tool. The best way to make money serve you is to *make it serve God*.

When we misapply that key word at the core of all that we are taught—*love*—by loving money, then wealth will become an evil that can consume us and set us up for a big crash. When "just a little bit more" is synonymous with one's self-esteem and identity, we are using the wrong scorecard. We look at assets as what will get us what we want in life—whether that be a better car or a fifth house on the Riviera—not what we are supposed to use to fuel fulfilling our purpose in the world.

So, let's say that how we are **RICH** is not how much we bank, but what we do with the money entrusted to us and who we become in the process of living out the purpose God wrote on our hearts? Let's redefine what becoming "rich" means in this context:

1. Responsible Management

The fact is, money is stupid. If we don't supervise it properly, it will get into trouble every time—and usually us with it. Money wants what money wants. It's up to us to tell it, "No, you need to do this instead."

In order to make money serve us, we must master it, which also means mas-

> The fact is, money is stupid. If we don't supervise it properly, it will get into trouble every time.

tering our desires, developing emotional intelligence, and building our identity on our relationship with God rather than pointing to what we have hoping to impress others. It means looking at our possessions in a twofold way. One is to look at what we have and say that "it is enough," and then proportioning it and allotting it according to sound money management principles and living within those confines. The second is to look at what we have and say "it is enough" to accomplish our dreams—at least for the moment. To see that we are actually well equipped no matter how much money we have is a revelation few manage. It means lifting up our eyes to see what God has really provided for us to get a job done rather than relying on money in the bank.

Wealth and provision come in many forms. Yes, in one sense, money is wealth, but so are relationships, talents, ideas, connections, skills, knowledge, materials, and so many other assets. We often don't realize all that we have available to us. Many times, we are one idea or conversation away from a breakthrough—it might be that person sitting next to you at church or that friend you keep feeling like you need to reach out to but keep putting off. It might just be a matter of starting something with what you have rather than waiting for the full-blown plan to be created. (A bias to action is rarely a bad thing, as long as you are open and comfortable to making corrections along the way.)

Yes, money needs to be managed to be mastered, but while money is an easy answer in a lot of situations, it's not always the best answer. That's why doing things *with* God is so important, and that is why the best decisions tend to begin with prayer.

2. Integrous Living

What good is anything if we are not living a life of integrity? *Integrity* is defined this way:

1. firm adherence to a code of especially moral or artistic values: *incorruptibility*

2. an unimpaired condition: *soundness*

3. the quality or state of being complete or undivided: *completeness*[10]

Or, as I like to simply say it, living with *integrity* means our actions and decisions must be consistent with our values, priorities, and principles, and those values, priorities, and principles must be sound and consistent as well. *Integrity* is a legacy word. Only what is built with integrity tends to last.

Here's a little secret: *There are no secrets*. We know God knows whatever we do, but so do others—or at least they will find out one day. People know who skims off the top, who isn't totally honest on their expense reports, who says one thing and does another, who doesn't tell the truth, who cheats at [fill in the blank], who looks at what is on their computer when no one else is around, who weasels out of paying their fair share, and so on and so forth. As you read this, I bet you are thinking of others you know right now who have high or low integrity. It's obvious to everyone, except them.

And, yep, someone else who is reading this might be filling in your or my name. You might say that they are weighing out our true worth. If so, how do we measure up?

3. Caring First and Most

I've already mentioned that those who care first and care most will always stand out from those who have other priorities. It's impossible to ignore them and it's impossible to not admire them. When we demonstrate caring, we deepen our indelible mark on others' lives. I'll go out on a limb here and say that as long as we care about others as much as we care about ourselves, it doesn't matter who the others are. Everyone needs to be cared about and for, in some way, and as long as when we care for others it is not to receive something in return, then we are doing the right thing.

4. Humility Wins

I like how Jordan Peterson defines humility in his poem, "Wisdom": "Humility is recognition of personal insufficiency and the willingness to learn." I think *pride* then, by contrast, would mean thinking we already know it all and holding on tight-fisted to all that we have.

We don't have to have a lot to share, and in fact, we don't really have to have a lot to be rich. One of our neighbors, Elsa, is so generous that when she cooks more than she and her husband need, we find a dish outside of our door. It makes me smile each and every time. She's an amazing cook and she's humble as she shares with us and others in our building.

Some very wealthy people are very humble. I admire those of them I have met. They open their homes and businesses to others, and they share their time, energy, and expertise, sometimes almost tirelessly. It's almost ironic that once we know this about people, we stop judging them on what they drive, where they live, how they vacation, what they wear, or whatever else they may have. Because when they share, we see their humility and the good works their wealth is serving.

Touching lives with what we have is the culmination of what it means to truly "be rich." And it is in this wealth we *"take hold of that which is truly life."*[11] Don't love money, love putting it to work for God and to benefit others, then you will be truly **RICH**.

REFLECTION QUESTIONS

1. Looking at what you hope to accomplish in your lifetime, how do you define the type of success you are striving for? What concerns do you have about your success? What is "your number"? How much is "enough" to earn in a year? In your career?

2. Read Luke 19:1–27. What do you get from Jesus's encounter with Zacchaeus? Why do you think Jesus decided to retell this version of the parable of the talents to cap his visit with Zacchaeus?

3. Read 1 Timothy 6. Reading the entire chapter, what do you think Paul was saying about wealth here? What did he mean by "the love of money"? How would you paraphrase his teaching to the rich (v. 17–19) and his instructions on the responsibility of wealth?

4. How will you plan to remain **RICH** as you pursue your dreams and calling in life? Describe how Rusty's four wealth principles apply to you.

5. Consumers tend to ask questions like, "How many seeds are in these apples?" while entrepreneurs and investors ask, "How many apples are in each of these seeds?" Are you a consumer or an entrepreneur? What does that mean for God's calling on your life?

NINE

FACING LIFE'S FAILURES

> And we know that for those who love God all things work together for good, for those who are called according to his purpose.
>
> —*Romans 8:28*

Face it. We (Rusty and I included) all mess up—and some mistakes are bigger than others. We all face hardships, and sometimes they are of our own creation.

Life has a way of catching us off guard, and if we're unprepared, we tend to make bad decisions. Even the wisest among us is unable to predict what lies around the next bend. When we think we know, we really don't. Just when we think we have the hang of something, we can be surprised at how much of it we can't control. One day we are sailing along, drifting in the gentle breeze, the sun is out, and life is good. Then in a moment's turn, we find ourselves under cloudy skies, with howling winds and ten-foot waves. Make one mistake in those conditions and you'll capsize. It has happened to me, and it's happened to you. It might not have been your fault, but when the pressure hit, you froze. You dropped the game-winning catch; something you said got back to a friend and was blown out of context; you fully intended to do something and got busy with something else, so it never got done; a coworker got called on the carpet for something you both worked on, and you didn't stand with her; you totally spaced the kids' soccer game. You failed to live up to the expectations around you, and even worse, you failed to live up to your own values.

How do we move forward when we have personally or morally failed? When we have betrayed a trust or someone's confidence in us? When such things happen, how do we push on without being ruined? How do we recover? How do we heal? What does God have to offer us in our pain?

The Bible is filled with examples of failure and recovery. In both the Old and New Testaments, there are numerous examples of people who experienced failure and recovered from it. In fact, one could argue that the overarching narrative of the Bible—and one that connects us to the mission of Christ—was God's recovery plan for the failure of the Fall. Genesis to Revelation reveals a story that goes from tragic failure to astonishing, comprehensive, joyous reclamation. Jesus talked often about how he came to seek and save the lost. He told parables about a lost sheep, a lost coin, and a lost son. He talked about how, by giving himself away as a representative sacrifice, he would pay the price that would redeem humanity from our bondage and pain—the ultimate redemption story.

What should this mean to us when we face failures and personal catastrophes? How do we start over? Or should we just walk away and cut our losses?

A CRUSHING BLOW

In reading the Bible, one man in particular stands out in my mind as a unique example of recovering after a rather personal crisis of character.

Simon Peter was a close friend and disciple of Jesus. On the night Jesus knew he would be arrested, tried, tortured, and eventually taken to die on the cross, he had a last meal with them in which he shared his heart and warned them of what was to come:

> *"You will all fall away because of me this night. For it is written, 'I will strike the shepherd, and the sheep of the flock will be scattered.' But after I am raised up, I will go before you to Galilee." Peter answered him, "Though they all fall away because of you, I will never fall away." Jesus said to him, "Truly, I tell you, this very night, before the rooster crows, you will deny me three times." Peter said to him, "Even if I must die with you, I will not deny you!" And all the disciples said the same.*[1]

G.C. Morgan, the great English writer and Bible commentator, suggested tenderly and insightfully that:

From that moment there was in the heart of Peter a consciousness that his Master was not able to trust him, a strange sense of distance between friends which is the most agonizing consciousness that can ever come either to one or the other. This man, knowing his Lord's attitude to himself, will endeavor to lessen the sense of distance by loud profession. . . . "Although all shall be offended, yet I will not." In that moment, Peter went further from Christ.[2]

From there, the disciples went with Jesus to the Garden of Gethsemane to pray—or at least for Jesus to pray. He left the disciples, and bringing James, John, and Peter, Jesus went further into the garden, asking them to watch with him. Instead, the three fell asleep. When Jesus heard them snoring, he woke them and asked them again to pray with him, even saying, *"So, could you not watch with me one hour? Watch and pray that you may not enter into temptation. The spirit indeed is willing, but the flesh is weak."*[3] Again, Jesus prayed, and again, they fell asleep. Then a third time, he woke them and returned to prayer. When he came back again to find them sleeping once more, he woke them just in time for them to see him arrested.

When Jesus refused to fight against those taking him, the disciples fled.

Jesus was tried before the high priest and the Jewish religious leadership. While this was happening, Peter sat in the courtyard outside the proceedings waiting to see what would happen. When a servant girl came up to him and said, "This man was with Jesus," Peter answered, "I don't know what you mean," and "I do not know the man." The third time, Peter even called curses down on his head and swore he did not know Jesus.

Then the rooster crowed. *"And Peter remembered the saying of Jesus, 'Before the rooster crows, you will deny me three times.' And he went out and wept bitterly."*[4]

Peter was crushed. Not just shaken, but broken, shattered into pieces. Peter's failure—like many of our own failures—was something he had been warned about in advance, and yet, still, he couldn't avoid it. Pride and fear had gotten in the way and undone him.

> Peter's failure—like many of our own failures—was something he had been warned about in advance, and yet, still, he couldn't avoid it.

The next day they crucified Jesus, nailing him to a wooden cross and making a pathetic spectacle of him. He hung there until he died and was then placed in a donated tomb. I can hear Peter trying to explain to the other disciples, "You don't understand—I *denied* him! I swore him off and he heard me, looked at me, our eyes met. I . . . I . . . there was nothing to say. He saw in me what I couldn't see myself—I loved my own reputation and identity more than I loved him. Now he's dead. He's gone. I forsook him. I turned on him. I should be dead—*I already am dead.*"

Days later, by the Sea of Galilee, Jesus would work with Peter. Even though Peter knew Jesus had risen and was alive again, he remained at his nets and fishing. We get the sense that even though Jesus was everything he had ever said he would be, Peter knew that he himself was not. He'd failed, fallen short of what God had called him to be. He had let a beloved friend down when his friendship mattered the most. He'd quit. He was content to go back to the way life had been before Jesus and make the best of his remaining years.

But Jesus had other plans—and those plans involved this very wounded disciple.

In John 21 we are told Peter and some of the other disciples had been out fishing all night and caught nothing. As they returned to the shore at daybreak, a man called from the beach, "Children, do you have any fish?"

"No," they answered.

Then Jesus repeated what he had said when he first called Peter, *"Cast the net on the right side of the boat, and you will find some."*

With nothing to lose, they did, and as had happened before, the net was so full it was too heavy to pull in. At this, John cried out, "It is the Lord!"

Peter leaped into the sea and swam to the shore to sit, so to speak, at the breakfast table his Lord had prepared for him. There is no doubt he was a broken man, happy to see Jesus, but torn up on the inside. He had briefly forgotten his pain in the initial excitement, but now the cloud had returned, and he had little to say. The boisterous disciple had receded into silence.

That is until Jesus restored Peter to his calling.

"Simon, son of John, do you love me more than these?"
"Yes, Lord; you know that I love you."
"Feed my lambs."
He said to him a second time, "Simon, son of John, do you love me?"
"Yes, Lord; you know that I love you."

"Tend my sheep."

[Jesus] said to him the third time, "Simon, son of John, do you love me?"

Peter was grieved because he said to him the third time, "Do you love me?" and he said to him, "Lord, you know everything; you know that I love you."

"Feed my sheep."[5]

Jesus was not interested in exposing Peter's failure, but instead gave him three opportunities for affirmation to replace his three denials. He wanted to heal it: to clean out and stitch up the wound. Before the conversation was over, Jesus was telling Peter that faithfulness was in his future, that someday he would prove to be valuable to God's kingdom.

It was a beautiful full-circle moment. The same one who had said Peter would fail when he felt so confident and self-assured was now saying he would succeed when he felt so useless and hopeless. The Master's assessment—something Peter had failed to trust the first time—was something he was being asked to trust a second time, albeit in a very different way.

That moment marked the beginning of a new chapter for Peter. In the end, after years of faithful service becoming a rock on which the Church would be built—as Jesus had foretold—Peter would indeed lay down his life, as a much older man, for the Lord that he loved.

What lessons are there for us in Peter's story? How can we apply them to our failures? How can we recover from our times of personal upheaval and defeat? A few things stand out, so let's talk about some key lessons from Peter's story:

When we fail and feel defeated, look to God first.

We all fail. We all fall down. But as the old saying goes, the ones who succeed are those who get up just one more time than they've fallen.

God's love never leaves us. He will never turn his back on us. Some of us may have a hard time forgiving ourselves for the things we have done and the people we have hurt, but there is no limit to God's kindness, forgiveness, and ability to heal us.

We simply have to trust in it and let him restore us.

In some situations, survival is a form of victory.

There are times when simply not running away or quitting in the moment of defeat creates enough space for things to calm down. Things rarely get better right away, of course. Defeats must be reckoned with, and the aftermath endured, but when we allow the poison to work its way out of our system without killing us, we are already paving the way for recovery.

Sometimes the best thing we can do is do no more harm. By resisting the temptation to compound a devastating mistake, we survive to live another day, and it's then when we find Jesus on the shore calling us over for breakfast.

Stay connected to others—don't isolate.

When we fall short and severely disappoint ourselves or others, we feel awkward and ashamed. The easier thing to do is escape that awkwardness by avoiding others altogether, and yet that is the exact opposite of what we should do.

Wisdom, strength, and healing come not from running away from the people who care for us but from choosing to lean into their love and encouragement even in our shame. So much of the recovery that God has for us is connected to others who directly or vicariously become conduits of his grace.

> Wisdom, strength, and healing come not from running away from the people who care for us but from choosing to lean into their love and encouragement even in our shame.

Trust God's promise that he can bring good even out of evil.

Jesus questioned and pushed Peter to reaffirm his love for him, and in so doing had him confess what he was not able to confess earlier. It was a small but important piece of healing, because what we affirm tends to grow into reality. Words matter; confession makes way to forgiveness. Grace and hope live in them.

Jesus invited Peter to believe that his words and promises were greater than Peter's weakness, sin, and failure. It was an internal struggle for Peter, but Jesus helped him see beyond his denial and cowardice in the face of accusers. Jesus showed him how he could turn shame into a humbler form of conviction and commitment. The Peter of the book of Acts is not the Peter of the Gospels. The brashness was gone, and his understanding of the power of redemption was much deeper.

So much of recovery is connected to believing God's words are greater than our own feebleness and shame. When we allow God's words to reside in our heart, they will guide us into a better future. Peter came out of his failure a better and humbler man, more Christlike, and more capable of inspiring and blessing others.

Our defeats can become God's victories. Peter's overall life shows exactly how that can happen.

AN APP FOR THIS:
CRISIS MANAGEMENT

If the last thirty years are any indication—the internet bubble bust of the late '90s, 9/11, the Great Recession of 2008, COVID-19, Russia's invasion of Ukraine, and so on—then major events that rock our world come at us less like a sine wave and more like an EKG readout—faster and more furiously. There's often no gradual rise or fall. One day the earth feels firm beneath our feet; the next we realize we just stepped off a cliff.

I've (Rusty) received and given lots of advice over the years on how to handle crises. What I am most certain of is that there is no one-size-fits-all solution. Like the hurricane chasers who fly their planes into the walls and eyes of a storm, we must collect as much data as we can before we decide on our next moves. We must ask ourselves what matters most so we can understand what we should do next.

When we interviewed him on the *Faith Driven Entrepreneur* podcast,[6] author and Pastor Jeff Henderson shared five questions to ask in the moment of a business crisis, but I'd go even further and say that these are questions we should be asking about potential crises as well—while the sky is clear

of clouds and the weather is fair. I know everyone has varia-
tions of these that they might use, but I love Jeff's questions
because they quickly get to the essence of moving from crisis
to the road to recovery.

1. What should we walk away from?

Remember my "love list" from chapter one? The fulfilled
life doesn't want us to hang onto every "love" we have accu-
mulated physically and emotionally. There will be a time to
purge and when better than before a downturn? It's easier
to make the hard decisions on what to throw overboard in
the calm than it is in the midst of a panic, so we don't really
need to wait for a crisis to address this first question.

But if we find ourselves in a crisis, then this is the time to
toss overboard whatever is weighing us down the most and
has the least use to us. We might have once loved doing something or owning something, but circumstances must be considered. We can ask ourselves what is it that hasn't really been
working. What's taking too much of our time without much
to show for it? What brings us negative energy or is resource
depleting? What just doesn't do anything to build us up anymore? Storage units across America are filled with things we
aren't willing to let go of but do us little, if any, daily good.

What we walk away from in crisis is usually well overdue.

2. What should we double down on?

There are areas we love in our lives from which we derive
happiness, fulfillment, and validation that it may be time to

give more attention to in a time of crisis. The COVID-19 pandemic kept us in our homes with our family and loved ones more than most of us have ever experienced, and we were forced to more than double down on our family time. While sometimes stressful and forcing us into things we didn't think we could ever do (homeschooling anyone?), we might just reap dividends from this time together for years to come, and maybe, just maybe, we kept and protected a little of that extra family time when things got back to the hustle and bustle of normal life. The same could be said for our exercise time, our reading time, and the friend time that we spent on Zoom.

Yes, there are areas where we need to double down.

3. Where can we take new ground?

A crisis, even one of our own creation, can also allow us to take new ground if we choose to push into it. One of the companies I advise had wild success with a webinar and was planning on doing one a month. Instead, they decided that if they upped the frequency and the level of the content, they might

> A crisis, even one of our own creation, can also allow us to take new ground if we choose to push into it.

come out of the backside of the pandemic considered thought leaders in their space. They didn't have to wait for the accolades, either. Within two weeks of beginning daily sessions, they were being pointed to as a company to listen to and whose advice to follow. They gained new ground a lot faster than they had imagined they could.

I'm reminded of the seafaring movies when the ship runs into an unexpected storm. I can almost hear the captain calling for turning the ship into the coming waves and wind with "All engines ahead!" The captain knows if they don't, the ship could get broadsided and capsize. There are certainly times we have to push into the storm to take the ground that is there to be gained.

4. What is essential?

Even in the worst times of uncertainty, we can boil down to what is essential for us at the moment. At the beginning of the pandemic, we all might have taken the essential nature of toilet paper too seriously as retail shelves were emptied— it became pretty close to being a commodity. We thought we were getting our "essentials" in order—to get a reserve of something we needed to weather the storm. In retrospect, I think we were concerned about the wrong things.

In a similar way, businesses that were over-leveraged with debt and didn't have enough cash on hand learned that being more liquid is going to be essential going forward. Any financial advice we are given from age sixteen on tells us that we should have three to six months' worth of savings in place for the "rainy days" of life. Warren Buffett likes to say, "When the tide goes out, you can see who is swimming naked." I'm not quite sure if this is the equivalent of a "moral failure" in business, but it certainly doesn't reflect wisdom.

If you're in a burning house, you need to know what to grab and what can easily be replaced later on. It's good to know what those essentials are long before you smell smoke, if possible. In business, it's good to know who you are at the core and what you can let go without compromising either your character or your mission.

5. What is possible that wasn't before?

Finally, "What opportunities are made possible by this crisis?" It's a very energy-creating, growth mindset, and motivating question to ponder. The answer for most is: "So much that we never thought about before and never would have if not for this."

Think about the churches that will forever have well-thought-out and robust online services and programs to offer after coming through all the shelter-in-place mandates. Consider whether or not we will want to talk to Mom or the kids over the phone anymore when it's now so easy to be video chatting with each other instead.

Like everyone else's, my gym closed during the worst months of COVID-19. I had a choice to make. Either I was going to discontinue my strength training, or I was going to make space in my home to do online training with elastic fitness bands. I'm proud (in a good way) to say that I was more consistent in my workouts during COVID than ever before. I converted my home office into my workout space (which takes me all of ninety seconds to set up) by rolling back my office chair and desk (on casters), securing the bands to the door frame hinge, and propping my phone on the windowsill so I can Zoom to see my trainer and he me. If you had told me prior to the pandemic that I should use my office as a "gym" a couple of times a week, I would have given you ten excuses why I couldn't and then gotten into the car to drive fifteen minutes to the gym and fifteen minutes back and felt good about it. Now I am thinking I might never go back to the old way. (I've since found an adjustable set of barbells and enclosed a small, neglected balcony area to use as a permanent workout space.) Yes, it's not the same as going to the gym, but there is no commute, the equipment is all mine, and there are no distractions for me or my trainer. In fact, I never really loved strength training, but now I have found myself starting to love my "gym" time.

So much of success in life is being open to what can be made possible. We are so fortunate that, in our lifetimes, technology has brought us so many opportunities to communicate, experience, watch, listen, and explore what we never could have imagined before.

> So much of success in life is being open to what can be made possible.

And all it takes to gain full advantage? We just have to be willing to question ourselves through the storm.

Yes, these five questions are simple, but also invaluable. They are good to keep handy, rain or shine.

Find yourself a place where you store the most important thoughts you come across. It could be a notes program on your phone or computer or a hanging file or a journal. Whatever you use, copy these five questions and the next time you think a crisis is beginning to brew, pull them out and spend some quality time thinking about what your answers to Jeff's questions might be. I can guarantee you that if you do, the power of the question mark will help build a new set of muscles for managing crises.

REFLECTION QUESTIONS

1. How would you say you operate in general? Do you live "hand to mouth" or do you have reserves to fall back on if anything were to happen? (For example, how did the COVID-19 pandemic or the Great Recession of 2008 affect you?)

2. Read Matthew 26:17–75 and John 21:1–19. Have you ever experienced something similar to what Peter went through in these passages? How do you think you would have reacted if you had been in Peter's shoes?

3. How was God with you through recent crises? What would you counsel someone going through what you went through in the midst of a rough time?

4. Today—whether you are in crisis or not—how would you respond to the five questions from Jeff Henderson that Rusty shared? Name three things you would like to change in the next week—and then in the upcoming six months—in response to your answers.

5. As we've read through and discussed this chapter, are there relationships you feel have been neglected or broken that you would like to repair as Jesus did with Peter? What's a first step you can take in the coming week?

PART IV

TESTING
THE FRAMEWORK

"A good tree can't produce bad fruit, and a
bad tree can't produce good fruit.... Yes,
just as you can identify a tree by its fruit,
so you can identify people by their actions."

—*Matthew 7:18, 20*

TEN

GRACE FOR
THE ROAD AHEAD

> God is able to make all grace abound to you,
> so that having all sufficiency in all things at all
> times, you may abound in every good work.
>
> —*2 Corinthians 9:8*

The call to be more like Jesus has never been an easy one, but if you've added some of the rituals and principles of the last nine chapters of this book to your life, you should be getting a little better at it. Our hope is that thinking of the faith code as a framework will make you better at loving the most essential things in life; you will be developing spiritual fruits which are, according to Galatians 5:22-23: *"love, joy, peace, patience, kindness, goodness, faithfulness, gentleness, self-control."* If I (Terry) were to sum these up into one word, I think that word would be "grace."

Grace is an interesting spiritual muscle, because it is what helps us remember to forgive—even to preemptively forgive, if you think about it, before the offense even comes—and it also gives us strength to endure. It keeps us from getting rattled when things try to knock us off course. It is what gives us the patience to give a soft, even-tempered answer when we meet anger, or turn the proverbial other cheek when someone tries to insult us.

Want a quick test for when you are low on grace? It's simple: "How do you react when someone interrupts you?"

Think about it for a moment. Don't answer too quickly. Is it with something other than a fruit of the spirit? Is it with something other than grace?

Now let me ask you another question. How did Jesus react when he was interrupted?

The first instance that comes to mind for me was when Jesus was teaching, and a bunch of kids wanted to come up to him. The disciples, seeing this as a disruption and annoyance, tried to head them off and keep the Master from being interrupted. Jesus's response?

"Let the children come to me; do not hinder them, for to such belongs the kingdom of God. Truly, I say to you, whoever does not receive the kingdom of God like a child shall not enter it." And he took them in his arms and blessed them, laying his hands on them.[1]

That's an incredible example. I think I would be more inclined to say, "Hey, can't you see I'm in the middle of something here?" (Yes, I know. I'm a work in progress, too.)

When you read the Gospels, you almost never see an angry Jesus, even though you will see plenty of times when he met frustrating people or could have been offended. The one real time that sticks out for me was when he rebuked the money changers and chased them from the temple because they were turning his Father's house of prayer into a *"den of robbers."*[2] In every other instance that he rebuked someone, I could see it being more even-tempered—more like a parent correcting a child.

Overall, Jesus walked in grace.

Rusty and I believe, no matter what your vocation or your position, if you are getting better at loving the activities, responsibilities, and people in your life, building up your grace reserve should be a natural outcome. And, because of that, you should begin to see it in your daily operations and interactions. Anxiety and anger should be replaced with peace. Forgiveness should feel easier. Setbacks and mistakes seen more as learning opportunities. Fear replaced with hope.

So let me ask another question: Where is grace showing up in your life? Is it guiding your interactions with others, as it did Jesus? Or is something else ruling your soul?

Those might be good questions to ask yourself every day.

WALKING IN GRACE

I know we just used Peter as an example of recovery from failure in the last chapter, but he also asked a great question that led to one of Jesus's best teachings on walking through the world guided by grace. This wonderfully instructive exchange is recorded in Matthew 18, where we read:

Then Peter came to Him and said, "Lord, how often shall my brother sin against me, and I forgive him? Up to seven times?"

Jesus said to him, "I do not say to you, up to seven times, but up to seventy times seven."[3]

Peter was likely greeted with a response that came along with not only a slight smile, but also a disturbingly penetrating glance, a glance that might suggest, "I know you think you have hit the target and that your broadmindedness is off the charts, but you are actually coming up short."

When Jesus said, *"seventy times seven,"* he did not mean a literal 490. No, it was a representative number that pushed forgiveness so far beyond the realm of sensibility that it could only be thought of as representing something more than a mere number. It would seem that Jesus was suggesting that forgiveness should be offered without limit.

The disciples must have been at least a little amazed having watched the exchange, but Peter was likely stunned and completely disoriented by Jesus's words. Again Peter, bless his heart, had thought he had pushed into the uncharted territory of being

> He had crunched the numbers, but Jesus blew them up, exploded the paradigm, and introduced a new one.

ridiculously generous. He had crunched the numbers, but Jesus blew them up, exploded the paradigm, and introduced a new one. It was as if Jesus said, "No, my friend, grace is too beautiful and bountiful to be reduced to numbers. There can be no limit to the spirit of forgiveness!"

An unforgettable exchange, but Jesus wasn't finished. He proceeded to tell them a story to drive the point home.

"Therefore, the Kingdom of Heaven can be compared to a king who decided to bring his accounts up to date with servants who borrowed money from him. In the process, one of his debtors was brought in who owed him millions of dollars. He couldn't pay, so his master ordered that he be sold—along with his wife, his children, and everything he owned—to pay the debt.

"But the man fell down before his master and begged him, 'Please be patient with me, and I will pay it all.' Then his master was filled with pity for him, and he released him and forgave him his debt.

"But when the man left the king, he went to a fellow servant who owed him a few thousand dollars. He grabbed him by the throat and demanded instant payment.

"His fellow servant fell down before him and begged for a little more time. 'be patient with me and I will pay it,' he pleaded. But his creditor wouldn't wait. He had the man arrested and put in prison until the debt could be paid in full.

"When some of the other servants saw this, they were very upset. They went to the king and told him everything that had happened.

"Then the king called the man he had forgiven and said, 'You evil servant! I forgave you that tremendous debt because you pleaded with me. Shouldn't you have mercy on your fellow servant, just as I had mercy on you?' Then the angry king sent the man to prison to be tortured until he had paid his entire debt."[4]

The story itself is one of contrast and sad irony. How could one treated so mercifully be so merciless? How can one forgiven so much be so unforgiving? But it's at least in part a story about how we are to treat people who hurt, disappoint, or try to take advantage of us. It's about our responsibility to extend grace to others, and about how that willingness to extend grace is to be informed by our understanding of how much God has extended his grace to us.

When we take an even closer look, it is impossible to miss the illustration Jesus is using. The picture is of a king settling his accounts and collecting his debts. One servant had managed to lose what to Jesus's listeners would have seemed like an enormous amount for their day—by some estimated as high as $20 million in today's currency. It is a fabulously large debt; something it was unlikely he would ever be able to earn or pay back in his remaining lifetime. What was at stake was everything the servant loved. According to the law of the day, his assets could have been liquidated and he and his family sold into servitude. Instead, he received mercy and forgiveness of the debt.

The way Jesus told it, the king was moved by compassion, so much so that he didn't even bother to consider a payment plan. It was a scenario where full restitution was unrealistic—either this man would be shown mercy, or he and his family would serve out the rest of their lives as slaves. The man couldn't make amends for what he had lost, it was just too much. The king allowed his heart to be touched, and in his pity, he chose to forgive the debt that couldn't be repaid—absorb the loss himself—rather than exact restitution.

It really is a picture of the enormous debt that Jesus Christ paid for us. Jesus did for us what we could never do for ourselves. He paid a debt, an incalculable, humanly speaking impossible debt with his own life. This is the essence of the Good News of Jesus Christ—we have been restored to relationship with God because the debt of sin that separated us is no more.

In other words, God took the hit, paying the debt we owed with the life of his own Son.

But Jesus didn't stop there. He pushed further still, by revealing what the forgiven servant did almost immediately after receiving mercy from the king. The way Jesus tells it, this very servant, after celebrating his great escape and with the forgiveness of the debt still on his mind, remembers that there were a few people he had loaned money to who had not paid him back. After finding one man who owed him a mere few thousand dollars—at least mere when compared to the millions he had owed—he proceeds to demand full repayment. When the man pleaded for more time, the former debtor who had just been forgiven had his debtor thrown into prison until he could raise the funds to pay him back in full.

It was a startling contrast. How could a man pardoned on the plank, so casually push someone else off?

When the news reached the king that the extravagantly forgiven servant had dealt harshly with his fellow servant, the king was astonished and angry. Jesus tells us that the forgiven servant was called in before the king to explain his callous and ruthless treatment of his fellow servant. The king didn't wait to ask for an explanation. He was incredulous and direct and with fury lacing his words, rebuked him, *"You wicked servant! I forgave you all that debt because you pleaded with me. And should not you have had mercy on your fellow servant, as I had mercy on you?"*[5]

Jesus's final detail drives the story to its devastating conclusion. The servant who had escaped judgment earlier was sentenced to an even stiffer form of punishment. In the ancient world, debtors were often tortured to try to extract unacknowledged sources of money. This man—this incredibly unmerciful, foolish man—was about to get the worst of treatments. And then Jesus sealed the story with a statement worth considering: *"So also my heavenly Father will do to every one of you, if you do not forgive your brother from your heart."*[6] Not torture in the exact sense but judge us harshly and hold us accountable if we refuse to be people who reflect the grace he bestowed through his only Son.

If that seems harsh, perhaps it is time to think about increasing our own ability to extend grace as we read of Jesus doing so often. Consider taking on some of the following mindsets.

Think of grace as a fuel that powers your daily interactions.

When we say a dancer is graceful, it means she or he moves across the floor fluidly, without impediment. I believe walking in *preemptive, premeditated* forgiveness causes us to move with a spiritual grace that should feel similar.

When we say a dancer is graceful, it means she or he moves across the floor fluidly, without impediment. The dancer seems light as a feather. I believe walking in *preemptive, premeditated* forgiveness causes us to move with a spiritual grace that should feel similar. Offense does not need to stick to us or weigh us down. Bitterness does not have to clog our arteries.

The more cognizant we are of how much we have been forgiven, the harder it should be to withhold forgiveness. This should cause there to be a grace in our steps and an eagerness to extend grace to others. I can think of no lighter way of living.

Sometimes it's best to start the forgiving process with modest steps.

For some of us, the thought of doing some of the things Jesus modeled—when he prayed to bless his enemies or advised that we "turn the other cheek,"[7] for example—is a height that we can never see ourselves getting to. And yet *"with God,"* the scriptures remind us, *"all things are possible."*[8]

And thus, taking that first step is exactly what we should do.

It may mean simply asking God to soften our heart, even a little, with our mustard seed of faith.

It may mean asking God to take away our ill will for someone, reminding ourselves of how much of God's forgiveness and mercy we have received ourselves.

It may mean saying something like, "Lord I place this person—whose name I can barely utter—in your hands, for you are righteous and just in all your ways."

These prayers begin the process of clearing our hearts of malice and opening up for future healing. When we do any of these, we are on our way to being free.

Forgiveness should be held in "truth tension."

Forgiveness should not be confused with not having boundaries. Forgiveness does not demand an instant return of trust. It does not mean there should be no accountability. Sometimes a situation is so toxic that the only way to start down the road of forgiveness will be to create distance in certain areas of your life or heart that person will not have access to, at least for some time.

Remember the Bible emphatically tells us God is on the side of the victim and the oppressed. He is just. He is very merciful, and he does not always give what is deserved. How grateful we should be for that! Because if we always got what we deserved, who among us would be left standing?

What having the grace to forgive does mean is that we should pursue peace and mercy. It means our intention and earnest quest should be to live increasingly without malice. We forgive the debt, so to speak, but we don't loan them more money. We release the grudges, but we don't expose ourselves to be readily hurt again. Forgiveness isn't a cancellation of wisdom; it's walking without the burden of malice and releasing the need to get even. It's living without the baggage of past hurts and prolonged grudges. It's living gracefully.

AN APP FOR THIS: EXTENDING GRACE

I like what Terry says here when he calls grace "preemptive, premeditated forgiveness" and goes on to say that living gracefully means carrying no baggage and walking "lightly" without impediment. Such a great ideal—but how do you live that in the typically turbulent everyday world?

Take, for example, driving in traffic—something I think we have all found frustrating at one point or another. In the Bay Area, we now share the same phenomena of brutal traffic as many of the other major cities in the world. Even though we are comparatively small in population, our traffic ranks right up there with larger cities. It was a couple of years ago that it was declared we officially no longer have "rush hours"—heavier traffic on the way to work or the way home—now it's just heavy traffic all day long. And with this increased drive time and slow-moving cars comes impatience and irritability. Suddenly everything that happens around us is amplified.

And I would be surprised if you haven't—as I have—"expressed" some form of unloving rebuke when someone cuts you off, does something inconsiderate, or whose aggressiveness almost causes an accident. It's not unusual to hear a horn blast and see an unfriendly hand gesture when someone doesn't like how someone else is driving. For some, this even emerges as something that has happened often enough now that we have a name for it: "road rage." It's amazing to think that frustration due to traffic has risen to the level of people being shot and killed because of it.

I mean, how far from grace have we wandered?

Why do I bring this up? Because it's something all of us who drive have experienced at least at one time or another, and, quite honestly, it's easy to see the ridiculousness of it. Some experience it daily, so it's not like it's unexpected, but they get just as upset. The essence of the meaning of the word *drive*, after all, is to exert effort or direct something toward a goal, whether that be driving a car to work, directing a team toward an accomplishment, or changing a paradigm in a marketplace. If something interferes with that forward progress, we take it as if it were a personal affront!

And my question is, *why?*

Anyone who has ever driven knows they are going to, at times, hit traffic. Some of us know it as a way of life. I can tell you without a doubt, crazy, offensive things are going to happen. It's part of living on this planet. It's to be expected. So, knowing it's going to happen, we can premeditate and preemptively choose how to react. We can meet it with frustration that explodes into anger, or we can decide to meet it with grace.

There's an old expression among leaders: "Never let them see you sweat." That doesn't mean to bury emotions when they come up, it means we should think ahead and prepare for them before they happen so that when they do, we can meet them as if they are just another pothole in the road— "Okay, that happened. We were sure to hit some obstacles. So, what do we do now? Is there maybe even an opportunity in this new development?" (Yeah, exactly! It's a perfect time to ask those five questions from the last chapter.)

> If we haven't strengthened ourselves enough in God to be able to overcome whatever the world might throw at us, we haven't done the right work.

In short, as leaders—whether we are leading from the top or the bottom—we need to develop grace for the road ahead. We need to do our workouts and stick to our rituals so we can be in shape—physically and spiritually—to run the unique race God has set before us. If we haven't strengthened ourselves enough in God to be able to overcome whatever the world might throw at us, we haven't done the right work. I think developing grace—through our daily and weekly rituals—is something God has called each of us to do. It's certainly something we see in the life of Jesus as Terry described earlier. It matches the kind of grace—preemptive, premeditated forgiveness—Jesus told Peter was required of us.

Can we truly be like Jesus if we never develop that kind of grace?

You might say it this way: "Grace is a mindset of love. It thinks ahead and prepares and does the work, so that when the unexpected comes, we can meet it as Jesus would." Grace is the measure of spiritual stamina we develop so that when we get hit, we can respond in love rather than in retaliation. It is the inner strength

> Grace is the measure of spiritual stamina we develop so that when we get hit, we can respond in love rather than in retaliation.

we develop so that we can do the second part of the Great Commandment: "To love our neighbor as ourselves." It is being adequately equipped to live by the Golden Rule: *"Do to others as you would like them to do to you."*[9]

Now let's take living by grace from our example of driving to work to being at work. (Yeah, I know, that's a whole different level.) What does grace look like in the workplace? How does it affect what is "driving" us as well as what we're "driving" to accomplish? What does it look like when a project is coming in late or over budget? When someone makes a mistake that means something will have to be done over? When a vendor misses a shipping date or runs out of stock of an item crucial to our production? What does it mean when a competitor underbids us and signs the client instead of us? How do we react when our boss berates us in front of the entire team or someone else gets the promotion we've been working overtime to get? Or any number of other things that happen in the workplace on a daily basis that are a possibility we could have foreseen but are frustrating all the same.

Just what does grace look like in those instances?

Most certainly, we should have grace, if for no other reason than it runs counter to our culture in the same way Jesus ran counter to his. It should be a mark of who we are that makes us stand out from the crowd.

Besides, as entrepreneurs know, it's sometimes in mistakes that breakthroughs happen. It is sometimes in finding joy where others experience frustrations that disruptive improvement takes place. In every traffic-jam-type problem, there is an opportunity for innovation waiting to be harvested (yes, flying cars are coming—I just don't know when!), and it is more often than not that someone with grace will do the harvesting, not the angry person who wants to shoot the person whose driving just offended them.

Think back to the capacity tests we talked about in chapter four: How we use our time, how we spend our money, what comes out of our mouths, and what we do with our authority. How does *your* grace show up in each of those areas? Do you have margin in your appointments so that someone who might

182

need your help can get time with you, or do you have time to just think and not be at the mercy of the urgent over the important? Do we take our "loving God" rituals seriously, or do we put them on the back-burner for something else? Do we live from overflow, with our inner tanks full, rather than running constantly on empty? Are we "graceful" in what we do with our money, living responsibly and generously so that we have more than enough to *"abound in every good work"*?[10]

> Do we live from overflow, with our inner tanks full, rather than running constantly on empty?

What comes out of us when we get news we don't like? How do we respond to emails, texts, Slack messages, or voicemails, when something in them upsets us or our plans? It seems to me that this would be a prime place to apply grace rather than express a lack thereof. It's easy to fire off a reply that can set off an avalanche of negative emotions and back-and-forths. When I see this happen or get pulled into participating in such a tirade, it always feels that the person who started it committed a self-inflicted wound. What could have been handled with grace has now turned into a hornets' nest of stung people.

How should we approach such moments as followers of God, *"full of grace and truth"*[11] as Jesus was? We are faced with such challenges daily, so we have plenty of opportunities to practice exercising grace.

That means, as we explored through the first three sections of this book, we need to be sure we have been internalizing the faith code and building on the framework of

God's love for us, his adoption of us, and his words to us. We need to establish the "subroutines" of loving God so that we have the heart, soul, mind, and strength to love ourselves and others. For when we are put in those life moments of pressure, frustration, and suffering that are inevitable in this world, we get tested to see if we will extend grace or collapse under pressure. Such moments can change the trajectories of lives. How will we show up in them?

REFLECTION QUESTIONS

1. Think about the last time you got really angry. Did you stuff it down inside, take it out on someone, or find a way to forgive, resolve the issue, and reconcile? How would you want to handle a similar situation if it happened tomorrow?

2. Read Matthew 18:15–35. Jesus puts a great deal of emphasis on forgiveness and reconciliation in the Gospels, why do you think that is?

3. How would you define *grace*? What do you need to do to be sure you have this grace in your life and be ever ready to extend it to others?

4. Which works best for accomplishing your responsibilities: grace or anger? "What would Jesus do" if he had your job?

5. How does "extending grace" relate to being vulnerable, being creative, handling mistakes, hiring and firing employees, or being a servant-leader where you work? What should a "graceful leader" or "graceful employee" look like in your everyday activities?

ELEVEN

THE IRRESISTIBLE ATTITUDE

"We played the flute for you, and you did not dance; we sang a dirge, and you did not mourn."

—*Matthew 11:17*

One of the great stories that Jesus gave us beautifully illustrates the value of an irrepressible, unrelenting, joyful attitude, and it does so at a number of levels. The story is perhaps the most famous of all Jesus's parables: The parable of the prodigal son.*

To understand this story, you need to understand its context. Jesus wasn't speaking to a group of prodigals, but a group of religious leaders who questioned his spending time with prodigals—the lowest of the low to them. The first verses of the chapter tell us, *"The Pharisees and the scribes grumbled, saying, 'This man receives sinners and eats with them.'"*[1] In response, Jesus tells a series of parables about things that

---

* If you'd like to read it in Jesus's own words, it is found in Luke 15:11–31.

were lost and then found. This parable, sometimes called "The Parable of the Lost Son," is the third.

Jesus always seems to color outside the lines the Pharisees and Sadducees drew for what was proper decorum and religious propriety. They were the models of self-control, but also self-righteousness. They had a whole set of rules and requirements for what pleased God without ever stopping to get to know God. As Jesus described their predicament at one point, *"You search the Scriptures because you think that in them you have eternal life; and it is they that bear witness about me, yet you refuse to come to me that you may have life."*[2]

On more than one occasion I (Terry) have called this "The Parable of the Two Lost Sons." At its center, most clearly, it illustrates the relentless and tender love of God. The image that Jesus presents us of God as an always hopeful, undignified father running to embrace the child who had fled him is powerful and profound.

Nehemiah 8:10 tells us, *"The joy of the Lord is your strength."* There is an attitude of expectancy that comes from loving Jesus and stepping into the life he wants to help us find. It is an irrepressible optimism that is anchored in the ultimate reality—the one God controls. Things may not always work out as we plan or hope, but, given the option, who would it be better to be like? The prodigal, the older brother, or the father?

ENTITLED? UNGRATEFUL? OR JOYFUL?

Most people want to make the prodigal the center of the story. Young, entitled, ambitious, and more than a little reckless, the prodigal son asks his father for his inheritance before he understands its worth so that he can go out and make something of himself while he is still young. As we will see, this younger brother clearly has some identity issues; he also has his loves in the wrong order. He is revealed as a young man frustrated by the mundane familiarity of his home, and perhaps tired of standing in the shadow of a prim and proper older brother. He wants to get out and stretch his wings, experience life, and cash in on his own wits and talents. He wants to make his mark in the world, so he goes to a distant land and starts living as if he's already achieved the success he aspires to, spending his money like it will never run out.

While the parable tells us nothing of the young man's aspirations, it's not hard to picture him as an inexperienced entrepreneur with a little too much capital backing and way too little actual planning to make his idea a reality. He seems to think he's got plenty of money to burn and the economy is always going to be good. His investment charts will always be up and to the right! He parties hard, enjoys whatever influence he can buy, and does painfully little thinking about securing tomorrow.

Of course, the story tells us how circumstances conspired against him. Not only does he run out of money, but he does it at the exact same time as an economic downturn, so suddenly there is no money to borrow and few decent jobs. There is no bailout coming. He's going to have to shut things down and find some way to support himself or he'll starve. Luckily, he finds something—the worst of the worst jobs for a young Jewish man—taking care of pigs!

187

When he finally decides to head home, he's ashamed and utterly destitute. He is very different from the brash young man who left home. He has experienced real pain and a loss of self-worth. He's certainly not the player he thought he was! His only anchor is his father, a man whose integrity he saw as he grew up in their household. He knows now that he was better off as a servant in his father's house than feeding pigs who, frankly, ate better than he did. He returns home repentant and ready to take any position his father has to offer because he knows him to be more just and kind to his employees than his pig-breeding bosses.

It could be argued that the father's reaction to his youngest son's return is a bit excessive. What about teaching him a lesson, or just letting him hang in the discomfort a bit so that he grows up a little? But wow! No lecture—just the ring, the robe, and the shoes, not to mention the celebration and the special feast. Not just a fattened calf. No. It was *the* fattened calf. The one they'd been saving for a very special moment. This was it! No holding back, cash it all in, time to celebrate! *"For this my son was dead, and is alive again; he was lost, and is found."*[3] From a spiritual perspective, Jesus was driving home the over-the-top, beyond appropriate, lavish, and, if one may say it, "prodigal" love that God has for each of us.

When the news comes to the older brother that his little brother has come home and his father is throwing a party for him, it is a hard, bitter pill for him to swallow. I can just hear him asking a servant, "What's all the ruckus about, what's going on? What's with the music and the dancing? How can

Dad do this? Doesn't he remember how my brother left—how disrespectful he was?"

When the father hears of his older son's reaction, though, how does he respond? *"Look, dear son, you have always stayed by me, and everything I have is yours. We had to celebrate this happy day. For your brother was dead and has come back to life! He was lost, but now he is found!"*[4]

Sadly, the son who left knew the love of the father better than the one who had stayed. The older brother thought it was earned, therefore was offended when his wayward brother's return was celebrated. The younger brother had realized that the nature of his father was quite different. You can't earn what is freely given!

This father loved both his sons *equally*. Just as he celebrated the return of the one that was lost, he went to the one who was offended. How each received that love and grace, however, was up to them.

If the Pharisees and scribes listening were to see themselves in the story, it wouldn't be as the lost prodigal, but as the older brother. When the older son hears the commotion and comes out to see his father pushing past decorum to express his love and gratitude for the prodigal's return, the older brother's only thoughts are that he is being slighted. He must have wondered, *Dad's making a fool of himself, and he doesn't seem to care.*

Exactly. Joy had taken over.

The older brother's attitude was the same as that of the Pharisees, Sadducees, and scribes when they saw Jesus eat with sinners. They thought they deserved the blessing the

Father was bestowing on the sinners—but their eyes weren't on the Father, who loved them as well. They were jealous of the blessings being bestowed and discounted the blessings they already had.

How the father went to both sons is a perfect picture of how God's love reaches out to each and every one of us. The older son was struggling to celebrate an incredible redemption. He was offended by the grace shown his brother because he felt it diminished his standing with the father, which, of course, was totally untrue. In a real sense, he didn't appreciate what he had because he'd never lost it like his little brother had.

How many happy moments do we miss on this side of eternity because we are angry or hurt, or because we've felt unrecognized for our faithfulness? The father reminded the older son that, if he wasn't careful, he was going to miss this special window of opportunity. An opportunity for grace, forgiveness, and celebration that had come like a gift into their lives.

> How many happy moments do we miss on this side of eternity because we are angry or hurt, or because we've felt unrecognized for our faithfulness?

A third perspective of this parable—different from those of the two sons—is the attitude of the father. He gets to experience joy because he never stopped loving his sons, even though his youngest had no doubt hurt him badly by asking for his inheritance so he could leave his family behind. He couldn't have been happy with anything his son had done. And yet, as Jesus tells it, when his father saw his wayward son, he ran to him with tears in his eyes. He embraced him and joyfully cried out that it was time to celebrate! When he saw his son coming back to him humbled and ready to be part of the family again, nothing else mattered.

Joy and gratitude are attitudes that keep us young at heart, reveling in the blessings of the present, appreciating the lessons of the past, and anticipating a better future. As we saw in chapter nine, Peter didn't find redemption from his mistakes until he could look Jesus in the eyes again and accept his grace, love, and the mission Jesus gave him to *"Feed my sheep."*

We don't have to wait until we make some colossal blunder like Peter did before we take on these attitudes—and I use the word *attitudes* here intentionally. Yes, love, joy, gratitude, and the like are emotions, but emotions come and go. Attitudes are things that we choose whether we feel them or not. The Bible tells us multiple times that Jesus was moved by compassion to respond to people who needed him, but he still loved them when emotion didn't move him. He was typically joyful and grateful because he chose to be. No matter what a person's past had been, when he saw that they were open to growing closer to God, he was slow to judge and quick to forgive, quick to be joyful or remorseful with them in their pain. Like little children who easily accept others and join together in play, God wants us to cultivate an attitude that is tender and loving.

So, when it comes to the attitudes we want to walk with every day, remember a couple of principles that will help you stay joyful.

Do not mistake being right with being righteous.

It's great to be committed and grounded to what is good and true. God wants us to have fixed foundations and a strong moral compass to guide our way. He wants us to love truth. We should always want to do good and not evil, as well as encourage others to do the same.

The older brother was right, but not righteous. Righteousness isn't getting all the answers correct, it's being in proper relationship with the Father.

> Righteousness isn't getting all the answers correct, it's being in right relationship with the Father.

The mistake the older brother made was that he established his identity on what he knew and believed, not on what and how he loved. Being "right" can make us judgmental and preachy and full of rebuke. Jesus only has rebuke for the self-righteous. Other than this, he rejoices at every incremental movement in God's direction or curiosity about who God really is. He chooses love over judgment and redemption over punishment, never compromising who he is.

We should do the same.

Cultivate a heart of wonder.

A child has a way of marveling over simple things that we adults take for granted. One of the reasons is they are constantly seeing things through a fresh lens, unclouded by preconceptions and cynicism. This ability to see and experience things freshly—a capacity to see the world with "big eyes"—is part of what fills life with wonder.

Jesus reminds us to ponder the lilies of the field, saying that *"Solomon in all his glory was not arrayed like one of these."*[5] He shows us that little things are worth noticing. Whether it is a swallow in a tree or a widow giving her last two pennies to the temple, he notices and rejoices in the wonder and remarkableness of the world around him.

Again, we should do the same.

AN APP FOR THIS: WATCH FOR THE EASTER EGGS

One of the little joys I (Rusty) experienced working for EA was that part of the culture was building little surprises into everything we did. In the videogame and entertainment world, these are called "Easter eggs"—little pop culture or throwback references to previous games and movies and so on or references that only the most attentive and well-versed notice and appreciate. (Sometimes they even include codes or other ways to access parts of the game or abilities those who ignore them will never find.)

They're called Easter eggs because when people find them, they feel like a kid finding an Easter egg at an annual hunt. They show up all throughout our media: in movies, TV shows, music, books, and well, pretty much everywhere. Authors drop them in like parents hiding eggs on Easter morning, hoping to catch a glimpse of eyes filled with pleasure and surprise when they are found. Pixar has built an empire on being masterful at giving us these little gifts that the adult laughs at while the kids think they are funny too, but don't know why. Easter eggs are like little gifts to us. To recognize an Easter egg in a game or movie is like being an insider—someone who gets the joke while everyone else is scratching their heads wondering what's so funny.

I think, in many ways, God has the same kind of sense of wonder and humor.

When God created the world and gave us his source code—and more specifically gets involved with our individual lives—I believe he dropped in a multitude of Easter eggs for us to find. The uninitiated, of course, will miss them, but I don't think that we should. Jesus spoke and taught in parables so that each of us could find a personal message and gift in his words. It was brilliant then and it still is today. We work individually and collectively to find the meaning(s) and then when we do, we are blessed with the gift of discovery and insight. It's like feeling the Father smile over us, which I think he does every time we get the joke or marvel over what he left just for us.

> When God created the world and gave us his source code—and more specifically gets involved with our individual lives—I believe he dropped in a multitude of Easter eggs for us to find.

If we refer back to our "Growing the Capacities" chart from chapter four, we can use the four growth areas as good places to start hunting for Easter eggs: Vocation, Recreation, Relationships, and Health. (Not coincidentally, you may also find that these are four areas where many of the things you would list as "what you love" appear.)

Vocation

Why are we good at what we do, and what makes us right for the job that we work? As we said in chapter four, underlying our calling are the talents, skills, and likes and dislikes that make us who we are. Could it be that these are gifts to be celebrated—and not just at work?

There is a continuing conversation I have with people who reach a point in their careers when they feel "restless" or "not challenged" in their jobs. (I have had this same conversation with different people so often that I can't remember how many times.) The person will have been in their current position or company for a few years and have been successful by many measures. They like the company. They like their boss. Their boss likes them. They like their coworkers, and that appreciation is shared. Their performance is good and well rewarded. But questions are bouncing around the person's head like:

"Am I growing and being challenged to my full potential?"
"Could I be doing more?"
"Should I be taking more risks with my career and trying something else?"

These are all good questions, but they are only the right questions if the person understands what is motivating them to ask.

What do I tell people who bring me these kinds of questions? The first thing I tell them is, "Don't throw the baby out with the bathwater." Having a good job, with people you want to work with, where you want to work and live, well that is a gift! Don't just change jobs and take on all of the risks associated with that move if you don't know why you're asking these questions in the first place.

Instead, consider staying right where you are and how you could extend yourself into outside areas like nonprofit boards, mentoring kids, volunteering in your community, getting involved in local politics, and the like. Maybe your questioning has nothing to do with your work and everything to do with your sense of contribution—stepping out into your community and helping there can be a great way of embracing new challenges and also giving back at the same time.

There is also usually more to celebrate about our work than we think. If our work allows us to earn a good living and take care of our families and future *and* leaves room for us to grow externally outside of our jobs, then there is a great amount to celebrate right where we are! At least it's definitely worth exploring before we make any other moves.

Recreation

When I was growing up, my father would punish my brother and me if we ever said we were "bored." His rationale was that we lived on a nine-acre farm with running creeks, a barn, a basketball court, and a go-kart track (with a two-seat go-kart!), and with all of that outside, how could we ever be bored? He was right. There was no reason. We just needed to engage our imaginations and get out of our self-defined rut. We had a whole world in which to explore and learn. Recreation is a gift we often overlook.

We must also recognize there are some who don't celebrate recreation time because they can't afford to have any, so instead they don't do much at all. There are others who are jealous of what others get to do, so their own recreation time in comparison never seems to fulfill them. Then there are those who just don't "play" enough because they don't want to try new things, or they feel more comfortable in their current routine. And yes, there are those who want to play, but do not live in a safe enough environment to do so outside of their homes. (Which is one of the challenges I wish those a little bored at work would take on!) But even in each of these situations, and they are real, there is recreation to be had if sought out hard enough.

For those times when we can *re*-create ourselves through play but ignore the ability to do so, we are looking the gift horse right in the proverbial mouth. Appreciating recreation time can be an Easter egg that keeps on giving if we only make the most of what is available to us, from volunteering to coach community sports to playing hide and seek in the backyard with our kids. To have thirty minutes a day to exercise or make our own play or movie with our family as the actors, go on a nature walk, or read on the train on the way to work—these are all gifts that come with time and the ability to appreciate (i.e., "make more valuable") what we are given.

Relationships

How often do we take those we know, especially those closest to us (remember the bullseye we talked about in chapter six?) for granted? If there are wonders to be discovered, they are in the people God puts around us. But when does that gift actually manifest? When we are with them and get to know them well enough to recognize the gifts God has put in them. Each time we engage with another person is a unique opportunity—an opportunity to discover a new Easter egg.

Truly appreciating others never gets old—particularly for them. Our tendency, especially as we age, is to keep the world small and make it smaller. I personally believe that approach is like receiving a gift under the Christmas tree and never opening it up.

The opportunity to establish and build relationships with others is all around us every day. It's in the Starbucks line, at the playground with the kids, in the lunchroom, on the train or airplane, at the conference, at church, anywhere there are people! Take a risk and take advantage of at least one opportunity a day to meet someone new—and never take for granted those who mean the most to you.

Health

We call it "the gift of health" because it is nothing other than a gift. We don't get to pick our parents and the genes that come from them and our ancestors. We do get to do the best with what is bestowed—exercise does improve what we've got—but that should never diminish being grateful for every healthy day and moment.

Health comes in the form of mind and body. Let's start with the mind. Learning and experiencing opens and betters our minds. Studies show that as we age, our mind, like a muscle, will atrophy unless we keep it exercised and stimulated. This cycle starts much earlier than any of us would like, and it's not surprising when we consider how our other muscles feel when they don't get worked out consistently.

Our mind is not something to let get flabby. We are presented every day with the opportunity to exercise our minds through reading, watching, attending, conversing, and listening. If nowhere else, the internet creates opportunities for us like no other generation before has experienced. But to learn is first to desire to learn.

I have a dear friend who likes to say, "You have to be present to win." To not look at expanding our minds through learning as a potential for discovering thousands of Easter eggs is to miss out on the full life experience. Most of us are surrounded by publicly funded places filled with wonderful gifts: museums, libraries, continuing education programs, sports groups, chess clubs, bridge nights, book clubs, free lectures, and so on. We can

> **"You have to be present to win."**

dig as deep as we like into the arts, science, history, and more. We can take free online courses that would have been cost and admittance prohibitive to us a few years ago. (Do you know what a MOOC is? If not, you should find out!)[6] Today, we can learn at whatever hour, whatever pace, and wherever we desire. Keeping our minds strong and sharp takes some commitment, but it is a pattern that can bring lifelong joy.

Imagine if we were all given perfect health and strong bodies that we couldn't tear down with bad habits but that would still wear out, and exercise, good food, and the like could not make them last longer. How would we treat those bodies? We'd probably abuse them like there was no tomorrow because that's part of our human nature to take for granted what we haven't learned to appreciate.

There's an old saying that leaders tend to spend their health to gain wealth, only to later have to spend their wealth to regain their health. Don't fall into that trap. Remember the story about the CEO/founder who didn't take care of himself until his co-founder got in his face about it? Let's not let ourselves get to the point of needing intervention. (Or think of reading this now as all the intervention you will ever need!) Let's keep our hearts wide open for the Easter eggs God has in store for us.

So, there you have it: Open your eyes every morning and start expecting to find the Easter eggs God has scattered throughout our world. There are so many little hidden things, woven into the very fabric of life, that God has placed there for us to stumble across, and hopefully each one will allow us to experience a moment of awe and pure joy. Think of them as opportunities to make God smile by getting excited by the Easter eggs he hid especially for us! Never stop celebrating and fully appreciating such gifts and opportunities, for, if we would only pay attention, we would see God's creation is full of wonders.

REFLECTION QUESTIONS

1. How would you describe the difference between joy and happiness? What kinds of choices would you need to make to ensure that your "joy battery" is "full" on a regular basis?

2. Read Luke 15:11–31. Which character in the story of the lost sons resonates most with you? Why?

3. How would you define righteousness? Does it have a good or a bad connotation for you (like "self-righteousness" does for so many)? What does it have to do with God's love?

4. Is there a way in the next month for you to practice more gratitude in your life? Figure out at least three and sprinkle them around on your "to-do" list.

5. Describe a time you discovered an "Easter egg" when you were open to something new and remarkable. What's a way to be more open to finding little gifts of joy that can help you grow on a more consistent basis?

TWELVE

PERSEVERING IN OUR COMMITMENTS

> Do you see what this means—all these pioneers who blazed the way, all these veterans cheering us on? It means we'd better get on with it. Strip down, start running—and never quit!
>
> —*Hebrews 12:1* MSG

There was a point in the ministry of Jesus when he was very popular. As I (Terry) said when we explored his relationship with Zacchaeus, he was enough of a celebrity that people would climb trees to get a glimpse of him. The disciples were overjoyed. They liked the crowds and the affirmation the crowds brought, but Jesus was unimpressed. He knew the fickleness of human commitment. He knew many were following him for the wrong reasons.

In Luke 14:25 Jesus is recorded as turning to them and challenging the "why" behind their interest. (We touched on this scripture in chapter six, but it's worth visiting again.) His words were not the way to build an audience, business, or create brand momentum. The disciples, it appears, were aghast at Jesus's strategy, for he challenged the enthusiastic crowd by telling them that they must hate—in this context, love less—their own lives and loves in comparison to following him. He pushed them all on the challenge and cost of followership. He asserted that if they were to be his sincere disciples, they would need to *take up their own cross.*

What he asked of them was alarming and symbolically alienating. The Jewish audience Jesus spoke to was well aware of the Romans' use of the cross as a tool for capital punishment. They had witnessed the brutality of Roman justice. To us, it might be like saying, "Unless you are willing to sit on an electric chair or be publicly hung, you cannot be my disciple," but even those pale in comparison.

Why use this disturbing symbol of death and suffering as a "recruiting tool"? Surely there must be a better way. While no one questioned Jesus on this, there can be little doubt that a stunned murmur filled the air. Then to this mixed audience of the committed, curious, intrigued, and recently offended, Jesus said,

> *"But don't begin until you count the cost. For who would begin construction of a building without first calculating the cost to see if there is enough money to finish it? Otherwise, you might complete only the foundation before running out of money, and then everyone would laugh at you. They would say, 'There's the person who started that building and couldn't afford to finish it!'*

"Or what king would go to war against another king without first sitting down with his counselors to discuss whether his army of 10,000 could defeat the 20,000 soldiers marching against him? And if he can't, he will send a delegation to discuss terms of peace while the enemy is still far away. So you cannot become my disciple without giving up everything you own."[1]

It was as if he'd said, "You cannot truly love me without paying the price of re-ordering your life. This is no small matter, no trivial detail. Weigh out what you are loving because it won't last if you don't persevere in it. Following me is a dangerously beautiful thing, and it will surely cost you something. So before you launch out with me and commit to my cause, ask yourself if you are willing—truly willing—to follow me through whatever may come. Will you stay faithful to the loves I have called you to?"

No, he wasn't making an appeal. He wasn't trying to remind people of what was in it for them. He didn't do as he had done on other occasions—talking about eternity or the abundant life. There was no discussion around the joy of being in relationship with God the Father or of the blessedness of sacrificial giving. Nor was there any mention of the eternal riches that come as a result of committing to him.

No, this was a "Before you sign, I want you to think about what you're doing" moment—and an "I want you all to understand what you are committing to and what it might cost you" warning. He wanted them to ask themselves, "Do I have what it takes to see love through to the end?"

IN THE BEGINNING, MIDDLE, AND END

Clearly the principle of counting the cost on the front end was a primary concern of what Jesus was asking here, but there were at least two other principles that should be considered as well. The first is exemplified by the king who assesses a situation and ascertains that warfare is not in his best interests because the odds are not in his favor, and as a result preemptively negotiates peace. This *principle of disengagement* is a reminder that in some situations wisdom requires us to shift our approach and settle for a less-than-ideal alternative.

Another principle—and the one that invites our focus—is the *principle of completion*. It has everything to do with the value of *finishing well*. Jesus's larger point was that we are not to commit to him rashly or ignorantly, but he also implied another truth, specifically that when a decision to start is made, we are to make a priority of fulfilling and completing what we started. It is important to finish well, especially when it is part of a commitment to someone else.

In the time of Christ, towers were typically built in vineyards to serve as vantage points for viewing and assessing threats such as fire, thieves, wildlife, and so on. They were often built high with a large foundation. There can be little doubt that Jesus's listeners had seen partially completed towers and other structures where builders had gotten part way through and then quit because they hadn't correctly calculated the cost of completion.

Sometimes in the process of building, as is still the case today, money would run out, challenges would be greater than anticipated, or a disagreement with the builders might bring everything to a halt. Perhaps the prices of raw materials went up, there was a lack of cushion or margin, an overly enthusiastic timetable got set, or even an unexpected downturn in the economy diminished expected revenues. Jesus said that the primary issue, in the case of his story, was a lack of foresight, a heedlessness that didn't think things through on the front end that resulted in quitting with the tower only partially built. Jesus declared it to be a testimony to foolishness. It was a clear warning against recklessness and emotionally driven commitment-making. He was calling people—to himself and to assignments his Father would give them in their individual lives—and he wanted them to see their commitments through to the end.

Called to the task of loving for a lifetime through the Great Commandment, there are several things we can learn from these parables:

1) How we begin and prepare matters.

Jesus was very concerned about beginnings. He wanted people to be clear-eyed about their commitments. On the front end of any meaningful project or pursuit, before we start, it's important to weigh things out, to prayerfully and thoughtfully consider our resources, our capacities, our strengths and weaknesses, our dispositional tendencies, and our motives—and double check our willingness to finish no matter what might come

> On the front end of any meaningful project or pursuit, before we start, it's important to weigh things out.

up. If not, we may find it hard to sustain our enthusiasm to the end of the commitment, be it to Jesus, a business partner, a spouse, a child, or anyone or anything else.

2) Every truly good and worthy endeavor will inevitably be tested by adversity.

In the journey of accomplishing any good work, rough patches are inevitable. Yes, nothing good comes easy. This is one of the reasons Jesus told us to count the cost. When it comes to things requiring commitment and sustainability, there will always be a cost. We will be challenged, and answering that challenge will require adjustments, honest re-examinations, continual upgrades, and even seasons of refreshing and renewal so that we don't lose heart. The greater the task, the more this needs to be taken into consideration.

3) There is a unique satisfaction and joy that comes when we see things through.

Most of us understand what it feels like to complete a short-term project: some task, a report, reading a book, a hike, a workout, or the like. It feels good to finish things we start. The longer the time to complete it, the better it tends to feel. Finishing a workout is great but running every weekday for a month feels better. And what about projects that take years, like building an organization or writing a book? (I feel a bit of it now as I write this last chapter!) The sense of culmination and joyful release that comes at the end of an extended effort is hard to beat.

Jesus, on the verge of finishing his assignment, the most difficult task ever undertaken by a human being, declared in his dying breaths, *"It is finished."*[2] His commitment to see his assignment through has changed the world more than any other action in history.

Finishing matters. We are told Jesus endured the cross for *"the joy set before him."*[3] The joy of completion and all that it meant to the Father and for us was clearly part of what motivated Jesus to endure such hardship, horror, and cruelty.

4) Both quitting and finishing can become habitual.

The more often we quit, for whatever the reason, the easier it becomes to quit the next time. Quitting tends to feed on itself. That is why there are some situations where we need to stay with our commitment even though we may realize partway through that we will have to overextend ourselves to finish. Maybe our reason for wanting to quit is because we have lost interest, or perhaps we feel marginally misled, or maybe we were reading things into the benefits of the commitment that weren't there. Remember, the mind can think of a hundred reasons to justify quitting—many of them legitimate—but that still doesn't mean we should quit.

According to Robert Roberts in his excellent book *The Strengths of a Christian, perseverance* is a "virtue by which a person is capable, and becomes more and more capable, of keeping commitments."[4] He also writes of "the ability to remain true over a rather long haul to an ideal, a commitment, a mission, a person, a job, when such remaining true is difficult because of besetting temptations, adversities, discouragements, and other changes of mood."[5]

Admittedly, not all commitments are the same. There will be situations where it is better to cut our losses and strategically disengage, but for the most part, if the commitment isn't unethical, irresponsible, or downright foolish, we are usually better off finishing than quitting for shaky reasons. There is a good deal to be gained in learning to persevere in our commitments. Some commitments are meant to be lifelong, while others are understood to be just for a certain duration. So let's talk about ways we can strengthen our capacity to endure when it gets hard to push on and stay on course.

5) Focus on the big picture.

When we find our enthusiasm waning, and we feel overwhelmed with the details, one technique for survival is to focus on the big picture. We should remind ourselves "this too will pass" and remind ourselves of the bigger goal that inspired us to make the commitment in the first place. Sometimes when we are feeling especially disheartened, we would do well to pull back and think specifically about how staying with our roles and critical responsibilities might affect others who are depending on us to be faithful.

Our choices affect people, and those people affect other people who affect still others. Sometimes just thinking about our children, grandchildren, and the generations to come can help us to hold tight when at least a part of us wants to run. What's more, seeing the big picture can help us when we are faltering and sense our grip weakening by reminding us that the present situation we find ourselves in will surely pass. One way or another, nothing stays the same.

6) Focus on the little picture.

There are times when the big picture can be daunting—when we are more than a little intimidated by the thought of keeping our promise for the long haul or an entire lifetime. In such cases, it might be good to switch to a smaller vantage point. Borrowing a concept from Alcoholics Anonymous (a concept AA founder Bill Wilson borrowed from the Bible), we can take the "one day at a time" approach.

We are not, as Jesus taught, to borrow from tomorrow's trouble. We may not think we will be able to sustain our commitment for a week, a month, a year, or a lifetime, but with God's grace, we can stay with it today. By hanging in one day at a time, we can prevail until a breakthrough or a deliverance finds its way to us.

> By hanging in one day at a time, we can prevail until a breakthrough or a deliverance finds its way to us.

7) Encourage yourself in the Lord.

This is another way of saying we are to bring our cause and concern to the Lord and trust him with it. The Psalms are full of prayers that echo calling out to God and claiming his promises as our own.

Also ponder the example of men and women in the Bible and Jesus in particular. In Hebrews 12 we read:

Do you see what this means—all these pioneers who blazed the way, all these veterans cheering us on? It means we'd better get on with it. Strip down, start running—and never quit! No extra spiritual fat, no parasitic sins. Keep your eyes on Jesus, who both began and finished this race we're in. Study how he did it. Because he never lost sight of where he was headed—that exhilarating finish in and with God—he could put up with anything along the way: Cross, shame, whatever. And now he's there, in the place of honor, right alongside God. When you find yourselves flagging in your faith, go over that story again, item by item, that long litany of hostility he plowed through. That will shoot adrenaline into your souls![6]

Looking to Jesus and how he modeled love, commitment, and sacrificial steadiness can inspire us to push on and not cave into the pressure. We can ask the living Jesus to help us by his Spirit to be more like him, to persevere and finish our assignments and commitments.

8) Choose to stay grateful, optimistic, and hopeful.

We can beat ourselves up over things we could have or should have done or said differently—there is a time to regret and repent—but there is also a time to accept and move forward. Write down some gratitude thoughts. Have fellowship with others and worship and sing to the Lord. Encourage yourself in his promise.

In the end, God is *always* for us. He is on our side, and he will help us to prevail. His ways are good, and there is nothing he can't guide us through if we will let him. His words—our source code—are life. We need to stay in them and always take them to heart. Whatever dark place we are in, he had his words written to light our way back to him and on into the reason he put us on the earth.

AN APP FOR THIS:
BEING READY

John Burke, the author of *Imagining Heaven*, profoundly states that our time here on earth is metaphorically just going through the birth canal to our next life in heaven. That begins to explain why, here on earth, we experience pain, suffering, injustices, and problems. I (Rusty) like the thought, because it just means that on the other side there is a new beginning waiting, and, like we can't remember the pain of being birthed the first time, we won't remember the pains of today, only the joys to come. I also like the metaphor because as believers we can say we were born three times before we meet God: once, our physical birth; second, our spiritual rebirth; and third, our eternal birth. In God's eyes, we are not a finished product when we die, we are only in transition for him to redeem us again.

> I also like the metaphor because as believers we can say we were born three times before we meet God: once, our physical birth; second, our spiritual rebirth; and third, our eternal birth.

So, I'd like to bring forth my final acronym: Be **READY**. We should always be readying ourselves for our future, both tomorrow and eternity, and one way is to remember these five points.

For us to be ready, we will have had to **Repent** of our sins and then live on with this repentance as a way of life. We have written about forgiving others with grace and why this is so important to being able to live fulfilled lives, but we can only be good at forgiving if we repent of our own mistakes and accept forgiveness ourselves. If we truly are appreciative of, and surrendered to, Christ because he forgave us first, then we can be the person who forgives others and treats others with grace. Being ready for the abundant life means being free from grudges and burying axes that should not be carried a day longer. We must not just be willing to do that with others; we must also be willing to do it with ourselves.

I cannot imagine a life that feels like it has ended well and is ready for tomorrow that is without **Empathy.** So much of what is swirling around us today and making things so hard on all of us comes from a place of not appreciating and understanding where we are each coming from. Do we even need to bring up politics to get the point? We talk past each other on social media looking not for commonalities, but only for our own way of seeing and thinking. We don't stop to listen. And, if we don't listen, we can't care. And if we don't want to care, then we become part of the problem, not part of the solution.

To change this is, by far, easier said than done, but we need to up our empathy. We all know someone who was remembered in their death for the listening and caring nature that they demonstrated. Spoiler alert: That is not just a natural gift that person was given. They had to work hard to develop it. If we are to truly be empathetic, then we must be able to walk in others' shoes. There are some things in life that we will never truly be able to say to someone else, like "I've been there," but we can say, "I'm here to listen if you'd like to talk things through." A little empathy goes a long way.

We can't just let our minds and worlds close in on us as they so want to do. We have to be **Accepting** in order to avoid becoming cynical, defensive, untrusting, or suspicious of others or what might happen to us.

An acquaintance of mine named John owns a landscape services company. John took over the company from his father and now has his son-in-law working for him, to whom he intends to hand over the business one day. John knows that time is going to catch up with his ability to push a lawnmower, climb a ladder, and haul away limbs and bags of debris. He's got some years left in him, but I have seen him spend more time doing the trimming with the powered weed whacker than cutting the grass. One day I asked him, "What did we ever do before we had those weed whackers?" John, said, "I got down on my hands and knees with a clipper and edged and trimmed." And with a lot of acceptance, he said, "I could never do that again." That is the *acceptance* of our physical limitations, of those things that, no matter how hard we try, will one day be out of our total control.

There are plenty of "out of our control" areas of life that we can respond to either by accepting and keeping moving on or by getting stuck and complaining about and trying to live in the past. People change. They change individually and they change collectively. We are part of that change too, and how we decide to grow through the change—or resist the change—will determine a lot about who we are. Considering this, the Serenity Prayer seems more poignant and timelier than ever:

God, grant me the serenity
to accept the things I cannot change,

the courage to change the things I can,
and the wisdom to know the difference.

Our tendency as we persevere to the end of anything is to try and "ease" our way over the finish line. I get that, as we know that there will be more to do, so we want to reserve energy and resources for whatever comes next. But I'm not sure that is how we are to finish each season of life well. I feel like we need *to* always be **Doing**, right to the end. If that is true, then the question is *what* are we doing, not *whether or not* we should still be doing it.

I think of Frances Hesselbein, who was still running her leadership institute and trying to affect the world for the better when she passed away at 107 years old. Her personal motto was "to serve is to live." I think my mother-in-law would agree. Into her nineties, she still volunteers at her church a few days a week. She called it her "job." She's never stopped doing for others, and doing for others is what keeps her fulfilled. Such amazing examples of purpose and giving truly inspire me.

There are too many stories of those who choose to stop doing what they love—or are forced to stop by either losing their jobs or for health reasons—and then they die. We are not meant to be like old elephants who just wander off into the jungle never to return. We are made to do and keep doing.

To be **READY**, let's always be **Yearning** for what is on the other side. Victor Hugo, along with writing the masterpiece *Les Misérables*, wrote "that the most interesting sound is that which is on the other side of the wall." Some would call that curiosity. I think it is more than that. I've always been

> I've always been interested in what is on the other side of the wall because I believe that there might be a life-altering discovery there if I only go check it out.

interested in what is on the other side of the wall because I believe that there might be a life-altering discovery there if I only go check it out. Now, that is not to say that I, nor anyone, should "experiment" with everything, but I will say that a strong desire to learn, discover, and be enlightened can lead to many opportunities and experiences we would never imagine.

We should yearn to learn more about God so that when we meet him face-to-face, we can connect even closer. This might sound silly, but have you ever checked out someone's LinkedIn profile or Googled them before you were going to talk to them on the phone or on a Zoom call? Of course you have. Why? Because you want to know as much about them as you can to make the conversation or meeting as casual and relatable as possible. We *are* going to be meeting Jesus at some point. Are we *yearning* today to know as much about him as we can so when we talk to him for the first time face-to-face, we are just picking up the conversation like old friends who never missed a beat? We should.

And God has told us to love not only him, but to love our neighbors. We will see them again too. Are we *yearning* to love them as much as we can before then? God makes promises to us about what we store up in heaven. Why would he do that if we won't one day tap into those promises for a joyous experience? So, yes, there are things we should be *yearning* for.

If you have gotten this far in this book, you are either likely to say that you are future **READY** for heaven or in a state of becoming future **READY**. These are great places to be because that readiness is just the beginning. And if you don't feel like you are ready, then there is still time. God is still waiting at your door to come in and dine with you whenever you are available.

REFLECTION QUESTIONS

1. What's a difficult relationship or situation you are facing at the moment that you've felt like you wanted to quit? Where might God's love and grace make a difference if you are willing to endure what you are going through and call on his help?

2. Read Hebrews 11:1–12:14. Hebrews 11 is sometimes called God's "Hall of Faith." It is filled with those who endured so that we might experience God's promises in a way they never did. How can you bring their examples into the situation you described in the previous question?

3. How would you define "playing the long game"? Considering the "quarter" of life you are in, what "mid-game adjustments" might you make? What do you hope they will accomplish for you?

4. Just how would you describe "winning" your game? What's going to make the difference between where you are now and when the final buzzer sounds?

5. When you finally meet Jesus face-to-face, what will you have to tell him about what you did on the earth?

YOUR FAITH CODE: A NEW BEGINNING

You learned Christ! My assumption is that you have paid careful attention to him, been well instructed in the truth precisely as we have it in Jesus. Since, then, we do not have the excuse of ignorance, everything— and I do mean everything—connected with that old way of life has to go. It's rotten through and through. Get rid of it! And then take on an entirely new way of life—a God-fashioned life, a life renewed from the inside and working itself into your conduct as God accurately reproduces his character in you.

—Ephesians 4:20–24 MSG

We've done our best to pack a lot of things to discuss into this short book and hope that you have enjoyed the journey with us. It is also our hope that you've made some friends along the way with whom you can keep the conversation going. There are so many different areas where it would be good to rewrite things based on the faith code. Our world needs Jesus as much as ever today, if not more so.

So, in closing, let us ask you one more time: "What do you love?" And, "How are you going to love it differently from this day forward?"

Our hope is, after reading and spending time with others in this book, that you've become more aware of how what we choose to love—even unconsciously—directs who we become. We are always growing—like a plant toward a light source. Too long in the wrong direction and we'll topple over and smash on the floor. For that not to happen, we have to be intentional about what we love and how we love it. We have to develop a rhythm among our priorities. We've got to design, apply, and test the framework upon which we are building a life. That's what the faith code is all about.

We also hope you have come to see that there is tremendous power in letting God work through your loves for his purposes. There is a world of blessing to realize. There are lives and livelihoods to be transformed. There is also an eternity to be won.

God is love and we are made in his image. We were designed to absorb and emanate his love because of its life-changing power.

While this is the end of the book, we don't think it should be the end of the conversation. We urge you to find a group at your church, at your workplace, at a coffee shop on a Wednesday morning at 7:00 AM, at a group like Faith Driven Entrepreneur or some other organization, to gather together and keep the conversations going about how to touch the world through better loving as God shows us how. Use this book, find a better book (there are thousands out there!), find a way to keep hearing and hearing what God is saying to us as his church and find ways to *do* what he is speaking to you.

That's the way to a flourishing life. That's the way to build it on solid ground. And that's the way to savor being alive. We think Paul said it well:

> *I'm not saying that I have this all together, that I have it made. But I am well on my way, reaching out for Christ, who has so wondrously reached out for me. Friends, don't get me wrong: By no means do I count myself an expert in all of this, but I've got my eye on the goal, where God is beckoning us onward—to Jesus. I'm off and running, and I'm not turning back.[1]*

Here's to it getting better and better and better as we go. God's not done with any of us yet. We should always be excited about what he has for us next.

We can't wait to hear your stories.

ACKNOWLEDGMENTS

FROM TERRY

This book is a product of a journey of many years. None of us is self-made, and in the end, we are mostly, from a human perspective, a product of our closest relationships. In light of that, I want to thank many of the people who have helped shape my life and ministry. In this unique way, all of you are a part of this book, and any healing and life that flows from my pen is connected to your love.

So I begin first and foremost by thanking the Lord Jesus, who touched my eyes when I was a young man and changed my life forever. My privilege is to follow you. My pledge by grace is to never turn away from the One who has the words of Eternal Life. For you are my savior, the gentle healer, my shepherd, my king, and my master.

Pastoring at Cornerstone Church in San Francisco, which I have done now for almost forty years, has allowed me to have not only the adventure of my life but also a laboratory for idea curation. Much of what was shared in these pages is a product of a love affair with Jesus and the church He has allowed me to lead since the days of my youth.

To all the people who have passed through the doors of the church over the many years and to a special group who has made the journey with me for decades, I say thank you.

To my mentors, starting with my first and only pastor who was also my grandfather Albert H. Brisbane, the man who fathered me in the faith as a teenager and into manhood, taught me how to love Jesus, and showed me how to pray. He was a shepherd who with little fanfare and only a modest harvest spoke to ten as if they were thousands!

To Jack Hayford, now with Jesus, whose counsel I received in countless conferences and pastoral schools of nurture. A giant of a pastor, radically spirit responsive, yet balanced and broad minded.

To Keith Green, you shot through my life like a comet and reminded me with your gift of song what "no compromise" could look like. My life was altered because of your blazing love for Jesus.

To Archie Webb and Steve MacFarland, two pastors who saw God's hand on my life and encouraged me to step forward and follow the call.

To my dear brother David Brickner, my backpacking companion, Ritual Coffee mate, and primary point of accountability these past two decades. Thank you for being a true friend. Indeed, brothers are meant for adversity.

To JR Castillo, one of the closest friends I have ever had, a man of war with a heart of gold; and to Phil Piserchio, the worship leader who has ministered alongside me for decades here in SF, and whose music and poetic gifts have made the journey one of joy and tears.

To Therese Robertson, my first hire and faithful ministry companion; and Odalis Turincio, an enormously gifted woman and emerging leader, a daughter in the faith, and a right hand in ministry.

To my only natural brother, Robert, whom I love; and my children, Caleb, Chloe, Jacob, Aubrey, and their spouses. Thank you for following Jesus. It has been the best gift you could ever give to me.

And finally, the best for last, the only true love of my life, the wife of my youth, Sheryl. How could I have known as a man of twenty-one that I found a treasure far beyond rubies? What a joy to make the journey with you.

FROM RUSTY

I could not have written this book without the encouragement over the years of so many faith-driven entrepreneurs and faithful readers of my Purposed worKING blog who seek greater purpose and meaning from their work and lives. Thank you to Henry Kaestner, Luke Roush, William Norvell, and Justin Forman who let me come alongside them at the beginning of *The Faith Driven Entrepreneur* podcast where I have been able to draw so much of this book from the amazing guests we have interviewed.

Terry Brisbane (as most importantly my Pastor) and David Brickner, thank you, for keeping me accountable and in our weekly "ritual" together.

And finally, thank you, Patti. Being a two-time author's wife and putting up with all that comes with it wasn't what you signed up for nearly twenty-nine years ago, but you've made it look easy.

FROM THE BOTH OF US

You wouldn't be reading this if not for Rick Killian. His mastery of taking our words and thoughts and turning them into a book was a marvel to observe. He's forgotten more about how to bring a book to life than we will ever be able to learn. We hope this is just the beginning of many collaborations.

Thank you to Gretchen Wanger, James Cham, Jeff and Alaleh Stecyk, Joe and Cecelia Gonzalez, Jonathan Petersen, Justin Forman, Ken Donnelly, Ryan Sanders, Sheryl Brisbane, Sue Alice Sauthoff, Therese Robertson, Tim and Chloe Cahill, and William Norvell who read the book in its infancy and gave us invaluable feedback.

Christopher Ferebee, you believed in us. Thank you! Phil Marino, your enthusiasm, and genuineness was what convinced us you were the right publisher and editor for us.

To the Team at CornerstoneSF Church, thank you for the support over the years of this book that emerged from our "LifeApps" Series and having our backs when you had to take on more to support us. We are so grateful.

Terry and Rusty

NOTES

INTRODUCTION

1. Proverbs 27:17 NLT.
2. Peter H. Diamandis and Steve Kotler, *The Future Is Faster Than You Think: How Converging Technologies Are Transforming Business, Industries, and Our Lives* (New York: Simon & Schuster, 2020), 236.

CHAPTER 1

1. Found in Matthew 5–7 and Luke 6:20–49.
2. Matthew 7:24–27 [emphasis mine].
3. James 1:23–25.
4. See Joshua 1:7–8.
5. Luke 6:48.
6. Charles Taylor, *Sources of the Self: The Making of the Modern Identity* (Cambridge, MA: Harvard University Press, 1989), 27.
7. James K.A. Smith, *You Are What You Love: The Spiritual Power of Habit* (Grand Rapids, MI: Brazos Press, 2016), 1–2.
8. Sanyin Siang, "One Million Followers Wasn't in My Obituary," interviewed by Henry Kaestner, William Norvell, and Rusty Rueff, *Faith Driven Entrepreneur*, ep 69 (25:20), August 13, 2019, https://www.faithdrivenentrepreneur.org/podcast-inventory/2019/8/13/episode-69-one-million-followers-wasnt-in-my-obituary-sanyin-siang-duke.
9. John and Ashely Marsh, "A New Class of Community," interviewed by John Coleman and Luke Roush, *Faith Driven Investor*, ep 119 (23:20),

July 25, 2022, https://www.faithdriveninvestor.org/podcast-inventory /episode-119-a-new-class-of-community-with-john-and-ashely-marsh.

CHAPTER 2

1. Ecclesiastes 2:11.
2. Mark 12:28.
3. Mark 12:29–31.
4. Mark 12:32–33.
5. Mark 12:34a.
6. John 1:17.
7. Matthew 5:16.
8. James 1:17.
9. See Mark 9:35.
10. Matthew 5:39.
11. Matthew 5:41 NASB.
12. https://www.faithdrivenentrepreneur.org/book-stories.

CHAPTER 3

1. John 13:4–5.
2. John 13:34–35.
3. See John 14:12.
4. Luke 10:25.
5. Luke 10:29.
6. What some refer to as the seven mountains of cultural influence.
7. Tom Morris, *If Aristotle Ran General Motors: The New Soul of Business* (New York: Henry Holt and Company, 1997), 94.
8. John 13:34.

CHAPTER 4

1. Mark 4:13.
2. See Mark 4:3–9; 4:14–20.
3. Mark 4:26–29.

4. Mark 4:27a.
5. Mark 4:27b.
6. Mark 4:28a.
7. Mark 4:28b.
8. Mark 4:29.
9. Mark 4:14.
10. Ecclesiastes 3:11 NLT.
11. Mark 12:29–30.
12. See Galatians 5:22–23.
13. See the often-ignored verses right before the fruit of the Spirit: Galatians 5:19–21.
14. Hebrews 6:12.
15. Carol S. Dweck, PhD, *Mindset: The New Psychology of Success* (New York: Random House, 2006), 6.
16. Ibid., 7.
17. Robert Green Ingersoll, *Abraham Lincoln, a Lecture* (New York: C. P. Farrell, 1895), 52.

CHAPTER 5

1. Mark 1:35–37.
2. Matthew 6:11.
3. Stephen Covey, *The Seven Habits of Highly Effective People: Restoring the Character Ethic* (New York: Free Press, 2004), 12.
4. Ephesians 5:15–16.
5. 1 Corinthians 9:24–27.
6. https://www.PurposedWorKING.com.

CHAPTER 6

1. See Luke 9:23.
2. See John 15:13.
3. Luke 9:25.
4. Luke 14:28–30.
5. 1 Timothy 6:19.

6. Dietrich Bonhoeffer, *The Cost of Discipleship* (New York: MacMillan Publishing Company, Inc., 1937, 1961), 47.

7. Ecclesiastes 3:1.

8. Psalm 90:12.

9. 2 Corinthians 4:16–18.

10. Gordon MacDonald, *Ordering Your Private Word* (Nashville, TN: Thomas Nelson, 1984, 1985, 2003), 7.

11. Martin Luther King, Jr., "Facing the Challenges of a New Age," January 1, 1957, address delivered at the NAACP Emancipation Day Rally, in Atlanta, GA.

CHAPTER 7

1. Timothy Keller with Katherine Leary Alsdorf, *Every Good Endeavor: Connecting Your Work to God's Work* (New York: Dutton, 2012), 34.

2. Ibid., 34–5.

3. Genesis 1:28 MSG.

4. See John 2:3.

5. John 2:4.

6. John 2:5.

7. Mark 11:22–24.

8. See Proverbs 8:12 KJV.

9. Colossians 1:10.

10. See Exodus 20:3–4: "*You shall have no other gods before me*" and "*You shall not make any carved images or likenesses*" to represent me (no idols).

CHAPTER 8

1. Luke 19:1–2.

2. Luke 19:3–4.

3. Luke 19:5–6.

4. Luke 19:7.

5. Luke 19:8.

6. Luke 19:9–10.

7. Revelations 3:20 NLT.

8. Matthew 6:24.

9. If you would like to listen to the talk, it is available at the Faith Driven Entrepreneur website at https://www.faithdrivenentrepreneur.org /entrepreneur-video/stewardship-vs-ownership.

10. "Integrity," *Merriam-Webster.com*, accessed June 12, 2020, https://www .merriam-webster.com.

11. 1 Timothy 6:19.

CHAPTER 9

1. Matthew 26:31–35.

2. G. Campbell Morgan, *The Westminster Pulpit Vol. I: The Preaching of G. Campbell Morgan* (Eugene, OR: Wipf and Stock Publishers, 2012), 195.

3. Matthew 26:40–41.

4. Matthew 26:69–75.

5. Excerpted from John 21:15–17.

6. Jeff Henderson, "Know What You're For," interviewed by Henry Kaestner and Rusty Rueff, *Faith Driven Entrepreneur*, ep. 108 (26:48–28:01), June 2, 2020, https://www.faithdrivenentrepreneur.org/podcast -inventory/episode-108-jeff-henderson.

CHAPTER 10

1. Mark 10:14–16.

2. Mark 11:17.

3. Matthew 18:21–22 NKJV.

4. Matthew 18:23–34 NLT.

5. Matthew 18:32–33.

6. Matthew 18:35.

7. See Matthew 5:39.

8. Mark 10:27 NKJV.

9. Luke 6:31 NLT.

10. 2 Corinthians 9:8.

11. John 1:14.

Notes

CHAPTER 11

1. Luke 15:2.
2. John 39–40.
3. Luke 15:24.
4. Luke 15:31–32 NLT.
5. Matthew 6:9.
6. A MOOC is a "massive online open course" that universities offer for free to anyone who would like to attend.

CHAPTER 12

1. Luke 14:28–33 NLT.
2. John 19:30.
3. Hebrews 12:2.
4. Robert C. Roberts, *The Strengths of a Christian* (Eugene, OR: Wipf and Stock Publishers, 1984), 83.
5. Ibid., 84.
6. Hebrews 12:1–3 MSG.

EPILOGUE

1. Philippians 3:12–14 MSG.